The Essential Nonprofit Fundraising Handbook

Getting the Money You Need From
Government Agencies, Businesses,
Foundations, and Individuals

By Michael A. Sand and Linda Lysakowski

CAREER
PRESS
Franklin Lakes, NJ

THE ESSENTIAL NONPROFIT FUNDRAISING HANDBOOK
EDITED BY JODI BRANDON
TYPESET BY DIANA GHAZZAWI
Cover design by Jeff Piasky
Printed in the U.S.A. by Courier

To order this title, please call toll-free 1-800-CAREER-1 (NJ and Canada: 201-848-0310) to order using VISA or MasterCard, or for further information on books from Career Press.

CAREER
PRESS

The Career Press, Inc., 3 Tice Road, PO Box 687,
Franklin Lakes, NJ 07417
www.careerpress.com

Library of Congress Cataloging-in-Publication Data
Sand, Michael A.
  The essential nonprofit fundraising handbook : getting the money you need from government agencies, businesses, foundations, and individuals / by Michael A. Sand and Linda Lysakowski.
    p. cm.
  Includes index.
  ISBN 978-1-60163-072-8
    1. Fund raising--United States. 2. Nonprofit organization--United States--Finance. I. Lysakowski, Linda. II. Title.

HG177.5.U6S36 2009
658.15'224--dc22

2009012607

Dedication

To the millions of nonprofit board members, staff members, and volunteers who dedicate their time, talents, and treasures to a multitude of worthy causes.

To the numerous nonprofit organizations CAPITAL VENTURE and SAND ASSOCIATES have been privileged to serve.

Acknowledgments

We could not have written this book without the full support of our wonderful spouses, Martin Lysakowski and Diane Sand. Special thanks also to our proofreader, Patricia Downing.

Contents

Preface

Why should anyone care about nonprofit agencies and their fundraising strategies? How many Americans are affected by nonprofit agencies and the decisions they make? Nearly every one of the million-plus nonprofit agencies in the United States is involved in fundraising activities. Whether the funds they receive come from individual donations, grants, United Way, or special events, they are involved in fundraising. As to the involvement of individuals, virtually every American is affected by the decisions made and services provided by nonprofit agencies. Individuals attend religious services, enjoy artistic performances, study in private schools, belong to civic groups, engage in recreational activities, get treated in nonprofit hospitals, and volunteer for numerous nonprofit organizations. Yet they often do not even think about the profound impact nonprofits have on their lives. The nonprofit sector employs more than 10 percent of individuals in the United States. In 2007, for example, more than $300,000,000,000 (yes, that is *billion*) was given to nonprofits in the United States over and above government funding received by these organizations.

As we write this fundraising handbook, the sky is falling. All four funding sources are experiencing major difficulties: government grants to nonprofits are diminishing, foundations are hurting because their funds are invested in the stock market, businesses in financial difficulties are cutting grants to nonprofits, and individuals in hard times are decreasing their contributions. Yet at the same time funds are decreasing, the needs of individuals for services are increasing rapidly. An argument clearly can be made that if the nonprofit sector failed, there would be an even larger impact on individuals than if the banking or the automobile sector failed. Yet we do not anticipate a government bailout of the nonprofit industry.

Many answers to this dilemma are outlined in this handbook. Greater cooperation in fundraising, better planning, and fundraising diversity are several helpful themes that will be discussed. This book will help overcome stumbling blocks to fundraising that result in many nonprofit leaders losing sleep. We hope organizations will benefit from our combined total of more than 60 years of experience in the nonprofit sector.

Introduction
Getting Started

More than one million nonprofit organizations in the United States raise funds from individuals, businesses, government agencies, and foundations. Many of these nonprofits are religious organizations (churches, synagogues, mosques, and temples). Others include educational institutions, healthcare facilities, human service agencies, arts groups, public service organizations, and many more. All segments of the nonprofit sector are facing increasing attention from governmental agencies (federal, state, and local), foundations, corporations, the media, and individuals.

Fundraising is an area that often attracts intense scrutiny. How much of a donor's contributions actually are used to fund programs? What percentage of an organization's total budget comprises fundraising costs? Does each donor's contribution actually get used in the way the donor intended? Nonprofit agencies must be especially cautious when raising funds. Transparency, ethics, and integrity are of utmost importance. It is critical for nonprofits to comply with all federal, state, and local regulations. Most states require nonprofits to register before engaging in fundraising. Many nonprofits, whether large or small, have trouble knowing where to begin when it comes to fundraising. First, many individuals do not understand what the term *nonprofit* means. A charitable nonprofit is usually a 501(c)(3) agency, a designation received from the Internal Revenue Service after meeting certain requirements—most importantly that the organization serves a charitable, educational, scientific, or community service purpose. Individuals can deduct donations to nonprofit organizations when filing their federal tax returns. Most government agencies and foundations will only make grants to nonprofit organizations.

Contrary to popular opinion, being a nonprofit does not mean that the organization must operate in the red or that it cannot have a fund surplus. The main characteristic that separates a nonprofit from a profit-making entity is that no individual or group of individuals can benefit financially from the profits of the agency. By receiving nonprofit status, these organizations are exempt from paying most federal and state taxes.

Nonprofits can get even more confused when fundraising "experts" give them conflicting advice as to where to begin. Many organizations that do not have professional development staff get caught up in a variety of activities that may not be appropriate for their organization, are time- and labor-intensive, and may not reap the expected financial benefits.

Though this book will be useful to larger organizations, it is written specifically for small nonprofit organizations with a commitment to service and not enough funds to fulfill their mission. These nonprofits must engage in fundraising every single day to keep the agency's doors open. We will refer to this concept as "forever fundraising." This is a reference handbook for staff members and volunteers engaged in forever fundraising.

Chapter 1 describes how to develop a fundraising plan. The other chapters are designed to help the agency tackle specific fundraising activities such as special events, proposal writing, and Internet fundraising. Once the organization has established a basic fundraising plan, read about more sophisticated approaches such as major gifts, capital campaigns, and planned giving. It is critical to resist the urge to race into fundraising without any planning—to decide to have a bake sale or send out a mass fundraising mailing. Those who have read our other books or attended the more than a thousand workshops we have offered will not be surprised to learn that we begin this book with the recommendation to Plan, Plan, Plan.

Include in the agency's fundraising planning (Chapter 1) specific roles for board members (Chapter 2), staff members (Chapter 3), and additional volunteers (Chapter 4). Most organizations make the mistake of developing fundraising activities and then feverishly looking for volunteers to perform needed tasks. For effective fundraising, first determine how many volunteers and staff members will assist. Then decide what the agency's fundraising strategy will be. Apply for grants (Chapter 5 and Chapter 6) as one part of an overall funding strategy. Remember, though, that nonprofit graveyards are filled with agencies that relied too heavily on governmental grants and could not raise funds locally when grants were not received or refunded.

Raising funds from businesses and individuals is a three-part process. First, identify the businesses and individuals you want to provide financial support. Then follow the tips in this book for getting them involved in your program. Finally, after they have visited the agency, read materials about its programs, or served on a committee, you can feel comfortable asking for a large donation.

Many nonprofits obtain much of their funds by asking individuals for donations. Because contributions from individuals account for approximately 85 percent of all philanthropic giving in the United States, several chapters will be devoted to the various ways of approaching individuals—in person (Chapter 8), by direct mail (Chapter 9), by telephone (Chapter 10), and through the Internet (Chapter 14). Each organization must make decisions about approaching individual donors. A good rule of thumb is to follow the 95/5 Rule: 95 percent of all contributions to any non-profit will generally come from about 5 percent of its donors. Those individuals the agency believes have the capability and interest to make major gifts should always be visited personally.

Another important rule to remember is that past and current donors are always the best prospects for a new gift. Loyal donors who give consistently and those who have a close affiliation with the organization (such as parents of current and past students or individuals who have used the organization's services) will be good prospects to be approached in person or by phone. Those whose interest is not determined or who could be thought of as "suspects"— those who *might* give—are generally best approached through less personal methods such as mail or Internet until their interest and ability to donate can be determined.

Begin by listing individuals and businesses that know about the organization and its programs. Divide the lists into three piles. Make personal visits to those likely to make major gifts to the organization (usually the top 5 to 10 percent of donors). Make phone calls to those likely to make medium-sized gifts (generally the next 40 to 50 percent). Send letters to individuals who are likely to make small contributions (all the rest of the donors and prospects). Of course, the decision of which names are placed in which pile will be affected by how many volunteers are available to make visits or phone calls. In addition to asking individuals personally for funds, this book includes tips for running special events (Chapter 11). Though they are labor-intensive, the advantage of special events is that, in addition to raising funds, they can be used to raise awareness of the organization.

Agencies are most successful in forever fundraising if they have a diversified fundraising program. A small agency can have an annual campaign, raise funds on the Internet, offer a planned giving program, and run special events simultaneously. As long as the total amount of net profits exceeds the agency's goal, it makes little difference if no single event is wildly successful. The first step in forever fundraising is to decide how much money the organization needs to raise next year. Notice, we said "next year" and not "this year." Most groups need to plan at least one full year in advance. Begin by making certain the organization has a well-functioning board and a strategic plan. A strong organization and a strong board of directors must be in place before beginning to raise funds. The next step is to review the agency's mission and programs. Many organizations find themselves spending time running programs that are not consistent with the agency's mission. The organization should honestly assess whether it is operating programs that other agencies in the community can run better or more efficiently. What are the current needs of the individuals in the community for the services offered? Be careful not to get caught in "mission drift." Too many nonprofits fall into the trap of chasing dollars from all sources for all programs rather than conducting their fundraising program to help fulfill their specific mission.

Next, see if there are ways to cut costs. It may be easier to cut costs than to raise funds. During the strategic planning process, it is critical to prioritize the organization's programs and then explore ways of cutting costs. Get several bids when purchasing major items of equipment. Take advantage of bulk purchasing discounts. Invest any unused funds rather than letting them sit in non-interest-bearing accounts. Compare staff salaries with industry standards. Prioritizing programs will be easier if the organization thinks in these terms: "If we can raise X amount, we can achieve these objectives; if we can raise Y amount, we can achieve these objectives."

Make certain every board member supports the agency. Remember that every board member must:

- Make a financial contribution to the agency.
- Volunteer in some way to help with fundraising.
- Attend the agency's special events.

Then, carefully think through fundraising options for the agency. One major variable may be the number and quality of volunteers and staff members who will assist with fundraising efforts. Read the chapter on staff involvement (Chapter 3) and the role of volunteers in fundraising (Chapter 4). Most effective continuous fundraising relies on the use of staff and volunteers, including every board member. Make sure all staff members are clear about the role they will play in fundraising and that these duties are spelled out in their job descriptions.

Another important variable is the likelihood of community support. Some communities have a strong businesses community; some do not. Some have a United Way that will support new community ventures whereas others prefer to fund more traditional, well-established programs. Some communities have numerous local foundations that support local agencies; others are more limited in the number and size of private foundations. Every community has philanthropic citizens, but these individuals may not be aware of the organization's programs and services. Often these philanthropists already have favorite charities they support.

Make sure the staff is trained in the latest fundraising techniques. For example, knowing how to use e-mail effectively and the latest techniques for Internet fundraising are essential to fundraising success.

In summary: Plan, Plan, Plan. Begin with the following:

- Solid programs that are needed and valued by the community.
- A supportive and committed board.
- A strategic plan with measurable objectives.
- Staff commitment to assist in fundraising.
- A plan for recruiting volunteers to assist with fundraising.
- A specific annual fundraising goal.

When these items are in place, the organization is ready to begin to plan how to raise the funds it needs.

Before beginning the chapter on planning, it may be wise to learn some terminology. *Philanthropy*, *development*, and *fundraising* are interrelated terms. *Philanthropy* has been described as a voluntary action for the benefit of humankind. In general, it refers to the entire world of giving, both from the perspective of the donor and the volunteers and professional staff members who bring about this giving and sharing.

Development refers to the process of developing relationships with donors that results in philanthropic giving and is the most common term used in the nonprofit sector to describe this process. Sometimes other words such as *advancement* or *institutional advancement* are used as titles for the individual or department that is responsible for development.

Fundraising generally refers to activities that result in contributions such as special events and proposal writing. In this book, all of these terms will be used. It might be helpful to think of the whole process as a concentric circle with fundraising as the narrowest circle, development as the next level of the process, and philanthropy as the broadest circle in which all fundraising and development is contained.

Chapter 1
Planning for Fundraising

"Cheshire Puss," Alice began, "Would you tell me please which way I ought to go from here?"

"That depends a great deal on where you want to get to," said the cat.

"I don't much care where," said Alice. "So long as I get somewhere," Alice added.

"Then it doesn't matter which way you go," said the cat.

—Lewis Carroll

Planning is critical in all aspects of managing a nonprofit organization. However, even organizations that understand the value of agency-wide long-range strategic planning often fail to use these same strategies in their development program. Fundraising is often done in a haphazard way because, like Alice, novices sometimes have no idea of where they want to be. They are caught up in the day-to-day management of myriad fundraising activities, many of which are often unproductive or counter-intuitive to the building of lasting donor relationships.

Undue pressure may be put on fundraising staff or volunteers by boards and executive management who think of fundraising as a "necessary evil." Despite the extensive body of knowledge on the subject of fundraising, these individuals still think of fundraising in the "tin-cup" mentality. They often refuse to make the necessary financial investment in a professional development office or the time commitment to develop an agency-wide comprehensive development plan. How many times has a well-meaning board or staff member attended a board meeting and offered this advice: "We should run a (golf tournament, gala dinner dance, art auction, walkathon, and so on) because (Girl Scouts, my church, the hospital, and so on) ran one and raised $100,000?" Before the meeting ends, the whole board is caught up in event fever and begins to discuss the invitations, the flowers, and potential T-shirt sponsors. What is the alternative to having the board being bitten by the event bug? Having a development plan in place is the answer!

Another fatal mistake many organizations make is relying solely on writing grant proposals to raise all the money they need for programs and operations. Given the fact that foundation grants only account for approximately 12 percent of all philanthropic giving in the United States, this approach seems equally as foolhardy as depending exclusively on special events to raise money for the organization. Although both grants and special events are important parts of a well-rounded development program, they should not be the only methods of fundraising used by nonprofits. So how does one handle these board suggestions or (in some cases) mandates?

Often boards and volunteers do not realize that special events and grant research can be costly, not only in terms of hard costs and staff time, but in opportunity costs. In other words, what activities must be dropped in order to focus the limited time available on this proposed new activity? The first reaction to the individual who has suggested a new fundraising activity should be

"Let's review our development plan and see if this special event or grant is part of our plan. If not, what other activities will need to be eliminated in order to concentrate on this activity?" However, many organizations do not have a development plan to review. This is one good reason why the agency needs such a plan.

Other reasons include the facts that the development plan provides:

- A way to determine the appropriate budget for fundraising activities.

- Assurance that fundraising activities provide a balanced approach (in other words, "don't put all your eggs in one basket").

- Assurance that the agency has the resources to implement the fundraising activities that are planned.

- Timelines that allow staff and volunteers to best utilize their time.

- A way to measure success of the organization's fundraising activities.

Organizations that have a development plan complete with timelines, areas of responsibility, and budgets will be successful at keeping the staff, board, and volunteers focused on the activities that are most cost effective and that produce the best results.

How Should the Development Plan Be Prepared?

Start with the fundraising staff person, if one is in place, and a dedicated board member who will head the fundraising committee. Add the following individuals to the committee:

- Several board members.
- Executive director.
- Staff members.
- Donors.
- Clients.

How to Develop a Plan

First, the organization must commit to strategic planning at an organizational level if fundraising planning is to be successful. Second, as the organization grows, it must allocate sufficient funding for a development office, allowing the agency to hire staff that has the ability and interest in planning for fundraising. In cases in which the organization is too small to have staff members devoted to fundraising, an experienced volunteer or group of volunteers must be committed to developing a fundraising plan.

Many of the techniques that apply to organizational strategic planning can be easily translated into fundraising planning. An analysis of the current fundraising program is a good place to start: Analyze the internal strengths and weaknesses of the organization's fundraising efforts and evaluate the external threats and opportunities for fundraising. Some questions should be asked to assess what kind of fundraising activities the organization should consider. For example:

- Does the organization have a base of donors who faithfully support the organization?

- Has a staff member been assigned to coordinate the fundraising activities?

- Does the organization have a compelling reason to support the agency financially?

- How committed is the board?

- How many other volunteers can be invited to help plan and implement fundraising activities?

Building consensus, a vital part of strategic planning, is also critical in the fundraising planning process. Involving key stakeholders in the fundraising program—board members, volunteers, management staff, program staff, donors, and development staff (if there is staff for the development program)—is critical. Just as in strategic planning, the development plan must be focused on the mission and vision of the organization. Each goal should be assessed in light of its relevance to the organization's mission and vision.

As with strategic planning, the development plan should focus on a limited number of goals in different areas. SMART (Specific, Measurable, Action-oriented, Realistic, and Time-defined) objectives should be listed for each goal. The operational plan also needs to contain strategies and action steps for each objective. A measurement system must be established. One individual must be responsible for the implementation and monitoring of the plan.

What Should the Development Plan Include?

The planning process should start with an analysis of current fundraising activities. Some questions to ask are:

- What has been the history of agency fundraising?
- Have results increased or decreased throughout the years?
- What are the costs of these activities, including financial costs and staff and volunteer time?
- Are there sufficient human resources to manage this activity?
- Is the technology needed to manage this activity in place?
- How do current economic and political events affect this activity?
- Are there ways to increase the effectiveness of this activity?

Once the current activities have been analyzed, a decision should be made to keep present fundraising activities, focus more time and energy on them, or drop them.

A solid development plan lists detailed objectives. Goals and objectives do not always have to be monetary. For example, an objective might be to increase constituent participation by 10 percent this year, to increase the size of the fundraising committee by four individuals, or to personally visit three major donors each month. Without specific objectives, it will be impossible to measure success of the plan at the end of the year and to plan for the future.

Who Develops and Implements the Plan?

How does the nonprofit organization find time for planning? Who will implement the plan once it is approved by the board? By involving the right individuals in developing the plan and then implementing it, the organization can move forward in a timely manner and provide a framework for evaluating its programs.

Typically, these are the individuals involved in the fundraising planning process and implementing the plan:

Chief Fundraiser

If the organization has appointed a staff member or volunteer to serve as the chief fundraiser for the organization, this individual has the primary responsibility for the plan. This individual will create a detailed fundraising budget. He or she also assigns responsibilities to those who will implement the plan. This individual will be held responsible for implementing the plan, evaluating the plan's success, and adapting the plan as needed.

Other Development Staff

In an office where there are additional development team members, they should be involved with the planning process and will implement the various segments of the plan that pertain to their duties. It is important to include support staff in the planning process; goals can suffer serious delays if support staff and technology are insufficient to implement the strategies to meet the objectives.

Non-Development Staff

The chief executive officer (executive director, pastor, administrator) of the organization may be the chief fundraiser. He or she should be involved in setting the goals of the development program. The CEO's role in implementing the plan, particularly the identification, cultivation, and solicitation of major gift prospects, will be critical in the plan's success. Therefore, the CEO must be willing to support the plan and to fulfill his or her role in the process. The chief financial officer (this might be the accountant or bookkeeper) must also be involved in the plan, particularly to budget for additional staff, technology, or other resources that will be needed to implement the plan. For some organizations, other staff members may be involved, such as program staff members who may be consulted regarding their funding requests and facility managers who might have capital needs that will require funding.

Board Members

The board is instrumental in developing a strategic plan for nonprofit organizations and should be involved in the development planning as well. Their role in developing all the details of the plan may be less intense if there is a development staff or a fundraising committee, but the board must be involved in establishing goals and objectives. Where there is no development staff, the board will be more involved in setting the details of the plan. In any size organization, the board's role in implementing the plan will be critical. Similar to the CEO, board members will have a key role to play in identifying, cultivating, and soliciting donors, so they must, at the very least, help establish goals and objectives.

Fundraising Committee

The fundraising committee will have a larger role in the planning process than the full board because this is their area of focus. The committee should include several board members and is usually chaired by a board member. However, it is important to expand the committee beyond the board and involve community members, especially those with community contacts and specific skills and talents that can be used on the committee. Include individuals such as an estate planning attorney, a financial planner, or an accountant who can help with planned giving. This committee, along with the staff, will play a key role in implementing the plan.

Other Volunteers

If other volunteers, such as a parent group, auxiliary, alumni association, planned giving committee, or events committee are involved in the fundraising program, they might also be invited to review and provide input into the parts of the plan that pertain to their activities.

Consultants

A consultant is often involved in the planning process, particularly in the assessment phase. Many organizations engage a consultant to conduct an assessment of their past fundraising performance before they establish goals for the current plan. A consultant can provide an objective view of the organization's fundraising program and help establish realistic objectives as well as recommend strategies for the plan. When there is no development staff or a volunteer experienced in fundraising, a consultant may be called in to assist in preparing the plan.

What Does the Plan Look Like?

One thing to remember about the plan is that it is more than simply a document! Both the process and the product are important. Whereas it is important to discuss who should be involved in the planning process and the process itself, it is equally important to produce a written document. The document itself will be critical to the evaluation process.

The plan should start with an analysis of prior fundraising efforts (assuming, of course, that the organization has done fundraising in the past). It should also state the mission and vision of the organization, because the mission and vision should drive all development efforts. The plan should then list the broad-based goals of the plan, specific objectives under each goal, and the strategies and action steps that will be used to implement the objectives.

A Word About Goals and Objectives

Many individuals confuse goals and objectives. Goals are broad-based items, such as: "Raise public awareness of our organization," "Develop a more effective board of directors," or "Increase donor participation." Objectives, on the other hand, are more specific and should be SMART:

- Specific.
- Measurable.
- Action-oriented.
- Realistic.
- Time-defined.

Objectives for the stated goals might be:

- To develop a Website that is frequented by 100 potential donors each month, by the end of the year.
- To increase the size of the board from nine to 18 individuals, throughout a period of three years, adding three individuals each year.
- To increase the percentage of donors who contribute through the annual phonathon from 14 percent to 25 percent in the next two years.

The Specific Steps

Each of the objectives should then include specific strategies or action steps to accomplish the stated objectives. It is critical to address these four questions for each objective in the development plan:

- Who is going to do it?
- When will it be completed?
- How much will it cost?
- How much will it raise?

All areas of fundraising should be covered in the plan, including various fundraising approaches, such as direct mail, grants, special events, telephone fundraising, and personal solicitation. The plan should also address the various constituencies that will be approached, such as foundations, corporations, and individuals—who may include alumni, parents, organization members, present clients, past clients, and community members—as well as organizations such as corporations, businesses, foundations, religious institutions, and service clubs.

The development plan, especially for organizations new to fundraising, should also focus on infrastructure that is needed to manage a fundraising program: technology, communications, research, cultivation, stewardship, human resources (including board, staff, and volunteers), policies, and procedures. A typical segment of a fundraising plan can be found in Appendix D.

Each objective must include the strategies and action steps to accomplish it as well as timelines, areas of responsibility, and budgeted costs. In setting goals and objectives, be sure to think about the SMART objectives mentioned earlier. Each strategy must be **specific** enough to be able to identify exactly what the organization is going to do in order to achieve this objective. It must be **measurable**—that is, the organization must be able to determine if it has accomplished this step. For example, did the board identify 20 potential fundraising committee members by August 31? It must be **action-oriented**, outlining a specific action that will be taken to achieve this objective. It must be **realistic**, yet visionary—not too easy to accomplish. There must be definite **time frames** that can be used to measure success. Was $10,000 received by March 1? Have 75 individuals made pledges by June 30? Did 200 individuals attend the annual dinner?

The planning document should be easy to follow, referred to often, and evaluated regularly. One of the biggest problems with many plans is that they sit on a shelf gathering dust. If the plan has all the necessary components, it should be easy to implement and easily measurable. Most plans fail because the organization is good at setting goals and objectives but not always as diligent when it comes to establishing the action steps necessary to implement their goals. The plan must be monitored on a regular basis.

Before the plan is complete, an evaluation process should be in place. This process will include assigning an individual, often the chief fundraiser, to monitor the plan on a regular basis. The plan should also include a section that lists all the action steps in chronological order, a section that lists each step that has a budget impact, and a section that outlines tasks by areas of responsibility.

If each individual, committee, or department that is responsible for implementing the plan has an easy tool to measure progress, it is much more likely that they will follow the plan. Similarly, the budget will be helpful when presenting the plan to the CEO, the CFO, or the board that must approve expenditures needed to implement the plan. Finally, the timeline, in chronological order, will make it easier for the chief fundraiser to measure progress on a monthly or even weekly basis.

At every fundraising committee meeting, the plan should be reviewed, especially in relation to the timeline and the areas of responsibility that relate to development department staff and volunteer involvement. The chief fundraiser should not use the plan to criticize staff members or volunteers who may be falling behind in carrying out their parts of the plan. Rather, the plan should be used as a tool to celebrate progress and discuss issues that might be impeding progress. Often segments of the plan are not accomplished according to the timelines. However, circumstances might justify this deviation. For example, a direct mail piece might not have been mailed on time because a major grant application took precedence.

The board, which also has a major responsibility for certain segments of the plan, should review the plan periodically to assess progress and help establish goals for the next planning year. The fundraising staff should discuss the plan with the CEO and outline progress made and areas that might be hindering implementation of the plan, such as lack of technology, inadequate board or staff involvement, or budget constraints.

It is important to follow established guidelines for various fundraising components that can help compare the organization's progress with acceptable standards in many areas. Remember that some non-monetary goals should also be established in the plan, particularly for organizations that are new to fundraising. Be sure to celebrate progress made on these goals as well. It is not always just about the money!

Try not to get discouraged if all objectives are not met. Looking at the plan on a regular basis will assure that some objectives are not totally ignored while other areas are being pursued. Staff, board, and volunteers must not be led astray by delving into areas that are not in the plan. If a good idea is presented that is not in the plan, the chief fundraiser should suggest that the idea be investigated further and possibly incorporated into the next plan. If the opportunity is immediate and the organization feels compelled to pursue it, then those involved need to examine the plan to see what area might have to be revised in the current plan in order to pursue this new opportunity.

One thing to remember is that the plan is not written in stone, but neither is it written in disappearing ink! It should be flexible, but not *too* flexible.

Chapter 2
The Role of the Board

Does every member of the board understand that he or she must be involved in fundraising? Does every board member understand that making a contribution to the organization's annual campaign is mandatory, not voluntary? Do board members attend the organization's special events and encourage others to attend?

If the answer to any of these questions is no, STOP. Do not proceed with fundraising until all board members are on board (pun intended).

Some basic principles that board members need to understand include the following:

- Board members are selected because of their dedication to the organization, so they should also have the desire to support the agency financially.

- It will be impossible to ask the public to support special events if the board members are not in attendance.

- Members of the community contribute more to an organization when they are asked by a volunteer whom they know than by a paid staff member.

- Ultimately, board members have assumed the responsibility for implementing the mission of the agency, and raising funds is a critical component of this responsibility.

"What do I have to do?" board members will ask. "Must I help with fundraising?" The answer to this question is yes. Though as volunteers they have a choice as to what specifically they would like to do to help, board members must support the organization's fundraising efforts. "Do I have to ask my friends for money?" The answer to this question is "maybe."

Here is a list of some possible tasks board members can undertake to help with fundraising:

- Serve on the fundraising committee to help plan fundraising activities.

- Develop and review mailing lists.

- Sell tickets for an event.

- Serve on an event committee.

- Ask friends and family to contribute to the organization in lieu of birthday, anniversary, or other special occasion gifts.

- Ask businesses to purchase ads in a program book.

- Visit companies to encourage sponsorships and contributions.

- Send an appeal letter to individuals they personally know.

- Contribute financially themselves (this is a "must do").

- Invite others to contribute.

Many staff members often ask what they can do to get board members enthused about fundraising. There are several ways to accomplish this goal:

- Help board members understand their role in fundraising.
- Assess the organization's fundraising activities and make sure board members aren't "nickel-and-dimed" throughout the year.
- Stress the importance of having a development plan that clearly spells out fundraising roles.
- Set up a strong fundraising committee.
- Select a board member who "gets" fundraising and have this individual chair the fundraising committee.
- Provide fundraising training for the board in specific areas as needed.
- Restructure the board to include more individuals willing to be involved in fundraising.

First, the board needs to understand fundraising and development, and what it does for the organization, as well as each board member's role in the process. Start by holding a briefing session at a board meeting; the board orientation is a good time to introduce this to new board members. Explain how important fundraising is to the organization and which programs need support from private donors. Outline the function of the development program and how the board and staff work together as a team to raise money. This is a good time to introduce board members to the fact that most giving comes from individuals, because many board members think the answer to the financial dilemma is to get grants.

Board Responsibilities

Every board member should have a "position description" outlining responsibilities to the organization. Among these responsibilities is the board's duty to assure that the organization is on sound financial footing, which involves not just monitoring expenses but also the organization's fundraising.

The board's special responsibilities in this area include:

- Understanding the funding sources of the organization and any economic and political trends that might affect these sources.
- Planning for a sound development program.
- Establishing gift acceptance and investment policies.
- Giving their own gift.
- Asking others to give.

It is important that board members understand the expectation funders will have of the organization. One question asked by many foundations and other funders will be, "What is the level of giving from the board?" Most donors will be reluctant to support any organization financially if the organization's own "family"—those closest to the organization—does not support it.

Creating a Fundraising Climate

Although some organizations do not set fundraising as a priority for its board members, most nonprofits can benefit from having board members actively use their connections to benefit the organization. The key to getting the board to embrace fundraising lies in three simple steps:

- Recruiting board members properly.
- Assuring that board members are committed to the organization.
- Removing the fear of fundraising that is common to many individuals.

Often, board members are reluctant to raise funds because they have not been recruited with that purpose in mind. Fundraising has never been a part of many organizations' cultures for various reasons. Perhaps in the past the agency relied on government funding, fees for service, or foundation grants. Then suddenly, when these funding sources shift priorities and income streams dry up, the organization decides it now needs to rethink fundraising and is stymied by how to introduce this concept to the board.

Even if the organization originally intended for its board to be involved in fundraising, many times board recruiters are reluctant to use the "F" word in recruiting for fear of scaring potential board members. Many well-intentioned individuals operate under the noble idea that "once they get on our board and see the great work we are doing, they will want to go out and ask for money." Wrong! If board members have not been told up-front that fundraising is a part of their role, they often will not embrace it later when the organization decides to slip it into its position description.

Recruiting the Right Way

One key concept to consider is *who* does the recruiting of new board members and *how* are they recruited. Instead of a nominating committee that meets once a year to fill vacant seats, form a year-round board resource committee. This committee can be called the board development committee, the governance committee, or any name with which the organization feels comfortable.

Whatever the title, the important things to remember about this committee are:

- It must meet year-round.
- It needs to be chaired by a strong and well-respected board member.
- Its duties include conducting an assessment of board performance, both for the board as a whole and for individual board members.
- It is responsible for developing or refining board position descriptions, which include a description of board members' fundraising duties.
- It evaluates the needs of the board and develops a profile of the kinds of individuals that are needed to fill board vacancies.
- It works with the entire board to help find the right individuals to fill board positions.

- It meets with potential board members and informs them of their responsibilities, including fundraising responsibilities.
- It assures diversity on the board, including ethnic, gender, geographic, and economic diversity.
- It implements, along with senior staff members of the organization, a board orientation session.
- It is responsible for the ongoing education of board members.

A board development committee can make all the difference in the world between an effective, enthusiastic, and inspired board and a lackadaisical board that does not understand its role in advancing the organization's mission. The latter will be reluctant to involve every board member in the fundraising process. One of the key roles of this important committee is to develop a board position description that includes a required financial contribution from each board member as well as the expectation that each board member must be involved in the organization's fundraising efforts. This would include attendance at events and helping to identify, cultivate, and solicit potential donors.

The board development committee should also help to assure board diversity, including:

- Professions.
- Income levels.
- Religions.
- Ages.
- Genders.
- Geographic locations.
- Ethnic groups.
- Length of time living in community.
- Skills and talents.

If the board has a diverse membership, the task of identifying potential donors is much easier. All too often, the board is not representative of the community it serves. Fundraising is much more difficult if no one knows individuals who live in a particular geographic community, members of a particular religious group, or individuals with large amounts of disposable income. This board development committee is also responsible for assuring that the position descriptions are not glossed over during the recruitment process. It must make sure that all potential board members understand that fundraising is an important part of their role.

The committee must be expected to deal with potential board members who are obviously reluctant to accept this responsibility. It is better to turn away a prospective board member who is not willing to get involved in fundraising than to fill a seat with a warm body just so the committee can say it has recruited a certain number of new board members each year. The reluctant individual may instead be invited to serve on a committee or in some other volunteer capacity rather than being invited to serve on the board.

Board Commitment: The Annual Board Appeal

Make sure all board members support the organization financially. Conduct a board appeal each year, asking each board member for a financial commitment. If the organization has several events planned, outline all the giving opportunities at that time, offering board members options for supporting the organization's fundraising activities (sponsoring a hole for golf tournament, buying a table at the dinner, or making an outright gift to support the program or operational needs). This way, board members are only asked once annually for a funding commitment, and the organization will know what support can be expected for the year. Stress the importance of board members asking others to support the organization. Brainstorm with them about whom they might talk to. Require board members to sign a commitment form that lists the ways they will support the organization and the contacts they will make on behalf of the organization.

Board giving is essential to show commitment. It is necessary for the board members to contribute to the organization's annual appeal for several reasons:

- It increases the level of "ownership" the board members feel toward the organization.

- It shows others that the board members are good stewards.

- It enables the organization to raise funds from foundations and other entities that ask "How much has the board given?"

- It makes board members feel good about their involvement with the organization and enables them to ask others for money.

Now that the need for board members to support the organization financially is clear, how much, when, and how does this all happen?

How Much?

Requiring board members to contribute a set dollar amount each year is discouraged for several reasons. For one, it limits the organization in recruiting board members who may have a lot of talent and skills but limited incomes. On the other hand, if the organization sets an amount, board members who could easily give more tend to give at the minimum level. Therefore it is better to stress in the board's position description that all board members are required to give at a meaningful level for them. The two key words are *all* (100 percent of the board should be giving annually) and *meaningful*.

When?

The annual board appeal should be completed before asking others to contribute. The best time to conduct the board appeal is at the very beginning of the fiscal year. For organizations that are on a July–June fiscal year, summer is a good time to gear up for the fall campaign. Having the board appeal out of the way during July and August puts the organization in a good position for the annual appeal and brings in necessary funds early in the fiscal year. Other boards solicit board members at the beginning of each calendar year and then ask for funds from others.

How?

The fundraising committee should determine how best to ask board members for their gift. A small group selected to solicit board members could include the board chair, the chair of the fundraising committee, and as many other board members as are needed to solicit board members personally. Individuals who solicit should be selected from those board members who are regular, generous givers themselves.

This small group of board members should evaluate the giving potential of each member of the board. Treat the board appeal as though it were any major fundraising appeal. Make it personal, challenging, and exciting. Generally, the organization does not need glitzy campaign materials for board members. After all, board members should know the reasons why funds are needed. Put together a one-page summary of the need for funds and a graphic showing the importance of the board appeal. This might include a pie chart with the annual fund broken down by categories (for example, how much comes from grants, events, mail, board appeal, and corporate donations). Another helpful tool is a list showing board members various ways their support is needed throughout the year. A menu of options for how they can direct their support will be helpful. It should always include unrestricted board giving.

Remember that the board appeal should be a serious effort including a personal visit with each board member, not just having the board chair hand out pledge cards at a meeting and say, "Okay, everyone. Make your pledge now." This latter method usually results in a much lower gift than making each board member feel special enough for a personal visit. A face-to-face visit also provides board members with an opportunity to ask questions and share their ideas.

Avoiding Burnout

If the organization is overly involved in special events, board members can easily get burned out. Most board members dislike being expected to sell tickets to their friends and family members for numerous special events. Many have no interest in golfing, running, dancing, or whatever the events involve. Focus on one or two successful events and stress the board's attendance to show the community that the board supports the organization. Involve the board in planning these events. Board members will be far more likely to commit themselves to support an event they have had a role in planning.

Stress to board members the importance of having a development plan that covers all areas of fundraising from events to major gifts and planned gifts. The fundraising committee should be deeply involved in formulating the plan and presenting it to the board. It is better to have board members ask other board members to get involved in fundraising than for staff to raise the subject.

Many organizations have succeeded in getting their board excited about fundraising by selecting the one individual on the board who most "gets it" about fundraising and having this individual chair the fundraising committee. His or her enthusiasm will be contagious and may even spur fundraising competition among board members. A consultant may be brought in to help motivate the board. As an alternative for organizations that cannot afford a consultant, inviting a board member from a nonprofit whose board has been successful at fundraising to talk to the board about their role in fundraising has also worked well for many organizations.

Getting the Board to Ask Others to Give

Time after time, organizations have been amazed to uncover some unbelievable connections on the part of board members who thought they "didn't know anyone with money."

The thing to remember is that every board member has a sphere of influence that can be used to help the organization. They just need to be made aware of the value of their connections and how they can use those connections. The following steps can help turn board members into movers and shakers in their own sphere of influence. (The same method can also be used with staff members to yield some amazing relationships.)

Schedule a brainstorming session at which board members develop a list of individuals they know who could be potential donors. It is important not to start them out with a blank slate. Giving them a blank sheet of paper and telling them to list people they know will result in getting back a bunch of blank pieces of paper. Instead, give them a list that will help them generate ideas. Ask them to list individuals who are their relatives, their neighbors, members of their religious groups, fellow workers, or their physicians or attorneys. Or give them a list of individuals who already contribute to the organization and ask them to discuss each name to determine who knows whom.

This process will help uncover connections that most board members do not realize they have. A good facilitator is needed to lead the board, such as a consultant or a board or staff member who has gone through this process. An experienced facilitator will be aware of privacy issues and organizational policies about what can or cannot be discussed within this group.

Is It Time to Fire the Board?

If all else fails, it may be time to look seriously at the board and restructure it to include more individuals willing to be involved in fundraising. Some tips for restructuring the board include:

- Make certain all new board members are committed to involvement in the fundraising process.
- If certain board members refuse to participate in fundraising, at the end of their term do not nominate them for another term.
- Ask the board chair or the chair of the fundraising committee to speak privately to board members who are not participating in fundraising and encourage them to do so.

- Plan fundraising training sessions to teach board members effective fundraising strategies and help them feel more comfortable with the process.

Note:

One important criterion to keep in mind is that all board and committee members MUST have a passion for the mission of the organization. If they have that passion, it will be easy for them to help in fundraising. In fact, they will be eager to do it!

Chapter 3
The Role of the Staff

For fundraising to be successful, all staff members must participate. As with board participation, staff participation must be carefully planned. Many nonprofits structure their entire organization to provide services but devote little planning time or staff time to fundraising. Too often, only the executive director or the development director spends time raising funds, and other staff members participate in a haphazard manner.

One concept that should be adopted by all organizations is that "fundraising is everybody's job." Raising funds should not be an afterthought or an add-on. Nonprofits should realize that fundraising must be a continuous, everyday part of their organization. Fundraising should be a part of every employee's job description. Staff participation in fundraising should be mandatory, not voluntary. Responsibilities for various aspects of fundraising should be part of each employee's work plan.

The job description of the executive director, the administrative assistant, direct service providers, and all other staff members should include specific fundraising responsibilities. These could include assisting at special events, identifying potential donors, helping develop the case for support, and creating awareness of the organization in the community. The responsibilities to develop fundraising materials and make phone calls as well as on-site duties at each special event should be spelled out clearly. Time must be allotted for the staff to assist with fundraising duties. All time spent on fundraising should be compensated and should be part of the employee's duties; staff members should not be expected to volunteer time to the agency.

Every staff member should be strongly encouraged to make a financial contribution to the agency, as is each board member, at whatever monetary level they feel comfortable. When an agency requests funds from a foundation or from individuals in the community, it is important to be able to state that every board and staff member has already made a financial commitment. Payroll deduction plans can help staff members make a meaningful gift to the organization.

Keeping Donor Records

One extremely important part of fundraising is keeping extensive computerized donor records. Start with basic information such as name, address, phone number, e-mail address, and the date each gift or pledge was made. Also include information on the nature of the solicitation. Was it made in person, over the phone, or by mail? Who was the solicitor? Include information such as contacts the donor has had with the organization. List relevant personal information including a donor's profession, marital status, age, and major contributions to other organizations in the community. A good donor software system should be in place, and staff must be given the support and training to manage this system.

Keeping Financial Records

Procedures should be instituted to assure that all funds are sent to the agency's office and deposited in a bank as quickly as possible. If a volunteer receives a check while visiting a prospective donor, the volunteer should mail or deliver the check to the office within a day of receiving it. The staff must keep meticulous records of all receipts and expenditures relating to fundraising. It will be crucial to establish a process for who receives checks, who opens the mail and records the gift, and when it is deposited to the organization's account. Financial accountability is critical to funders. The organization must have clear policies to prevent fraud and waste.

Producing Fiscal Reports

The staff must prepare accurate reports of how much money was pledged and received. The reports should also include detailed reports of expenditures. For example, a financial report on a fundraising dinner should include not only receipts but also all expenditures relating to the dinner, including printing, mailing, duplicating, and food costs. All too often, only the receipts of a special event are reported but not the expenditures.

Maintaining Volunteer Reports

A system should be established for keeping careful records of volunteer work. Records should indicate specific tasks each volunteer performed relating to each fundraising event and the amount of volunteer time that was contributed to the organization. Often, volunteer hours can be counted as in-kind contributions to the organization when applying for grants.

Keeping Meeting Minutes

Staff members should make sure that records are kept of each meeting relating to fundraising (including specific assignments that were made) and that these records are distributed to committee members on a timely basis.

Keeping Master Copies of Fundraising Documents

The staff should make certain to keep original copies of flyers, posters, mailings, and other documents relating to the fundraising campaign, both in hard copy and on the computer. When future campaigns are planned, existing documents can be revised as needed.

Sending Out Merged Letters

It is a major time-saving device for the staff to prepare letters on the computer and handle the bulk mail process. Letters confirming pledges, for example, should be sent out by the staff even though they should be signed by the volunteer making the solicitation. Donor software systems will have the capability of preparing merged mail letters, which will save time while maintaining a personalized approach.

The Role of the Executive Director

Every nonprofit should carefully review the duties of the executive director. It is essential to develop the right balance between the fundraising and other duties of the executive director. To the extent possible, the executive director should concentrate on fulfilling the mission of the agency, but must spend sufficient time on fundraising. He or she must feel comfortable with fundraising. The executive director is the "face" of the organization, and most chief executive officers of businesses and foundations will expect to meet with the CEO of the nonprofit.

The executive director has certain duties relating to fundraising:

- **Assigning duties to staff:** It is the executive director's responsibility to ensure that the staff members are carrying out their fundraising duties.

- **Serving as liaison with the board:** The executive director should report on staff fundraising activities at board meetings unless there is a development staff person who will assume this responsibility.

- **Representing the staff at meetings of the fundraising committee:** In smaller organizations, the executive director serves as a member of the fundraising committee. In larger organizations, a development director can serve in this capacity.

- **Representing the organization in the community:** The most successful organizations have executive directors who are active in local civic and professional groups in their community.

- **Meeting with major donors:** Individuals, businesses, and foundations considering a major gift will usually want to "hear it from the top" when being presented with a request for funding.

The Role of the Development Director

As the organization grows, it is strongly encouraged to hire a full-time or at least a part-time development director. This is a professional position for an individual with training and experience in the fundraising field. It is important to stress that the development director serves as the chief planner, organizer, and advisor to the board, staff, and non-board volunteers in the fundraising efforts of the agency. Often when an organization hires a development director, the board and other staff members fail to perform their fundraising responsibilities. They think incorrectly that the development director's role is to perform all the agency's fundraising tasks. Do not make this mistake. The development director should develop a plan to train board members in various fundraising techniques. The development director should only solicit contributions when he or she has a personal relationship with the donor.

Staff Enthusiasm

It is important for staff members to be enthusiastic about their fundraising roles. If they are dedicated to the mission of the agency, they will realize that only through fundraising can the agency succeed in meeting its goals. No funds, no jobs.

Chapter 4
Involving Volunteers

Can volunteers be effective in fundraising? Who can be recruited to serve as volunteer fundraisers? How do these volunteers receive the training and information they need to be effective fundraisers? The answers to these questions will vary from organization to organization. However, every nonprofit organization will benefit from involving volunteers in addition to board and staff members in fundraising activities. The key is learning how to recruit the right volunteers for the right job and to provide these volunteers with the tools they need in order to be effective fundraisers.

Many individuals feel that volunteers are the best advocates for an organization. It is important for a nonprofit to prove its credibility by showing the ability to recruit volunteer fundraisers.

Some cardinal rules of involving volunteers in fundraising are:

- Volunteers will only be effective if they truly believe in the mission of the organization.
- Volunteers should be invited to give of their time, talent, and treasure.
- Volunteers must be given meaningful work, not just "busy work."
- Volunteers require staff support in order to be effective.

As donors do, volunteers become involved for many reasons, including their own family history, religious influence, altruism, wanting to give back, community spirit, investing in their own or someone else's future, or because it is fun. If they do not believe in the mission of the organization, however, they will not be effective volunteers who can successfully ask a potential donor to contribute to the organization.

Who is the ideal volunteer?

- Someone who is committed to the mission of the organization.
- Someone who has connections to individuals who cannot be reached otherwise.
- Someone who can commit the time to helping the organization.

What is needed to keep volunteers involved?

- Expectations that are clearly communicated.
- Tools that will enable the volunteer to succeed.
- Acknowledgment that the volunteer role is important to the organization.

What qualities should a volunteer fundraiser possess?

- Integrity, in order to gain the trust of potential donors.
- Good listening skills.
- The ability to inspire and motivate others to action.

- Willingness to learn new skills and to accept new responsibilities.
- A caring attitude toward people.

The time commitment can be extensive, but experience shows that those who really care about a cause will find the time to devote to it.

Fundraising Roles for Volunteers

Numerous fundraising activities can effectively use volunteers, such as:

- Special events.
- Direct mail.
- Telephone fundraising.
- Corporate appeals.
- Grant proposals.
- Major gifts appeals.
- Capital and endowment campaigns.
- Planned giving efforts.

Though some of these activities are traditionally known to be volunteer-dependent, all of these areas can effectively use volunteers.

Why Volunteers Are Effective at Making the "Ask"

Volunteers are in a unique position to ask others for money for several reasons. They:

- Are not getting paid to do it.
- Have a real commitment to the mission of the organization.
- Have already made a contribution themselves.
- Care enough that they are taking time to participate in the nonprofit organization's fundraising program.
- Are doing a task for which they recognize a need.
- Generally have strong relationships with potential donors.

One of the reasons volunteers are so good at asking for money is simply that they *are* volunteers. Another reason volunteers can be more effective than staff is that they are usually soliciting their peers and approaching people to give at a level at which they themselves have already given.

Volunteers play a critical role in fundraising. They bring sincerity and commitment to the table. They often have connections that would not be available to the nonprofit fundraiser. Their special expertise and leadership qualities lend credibility to the organization.

Finding Volunteer Fundraisers

Volunteers, as with major donors, do not drop from the sky. The volunteer recruitment process is the first step in building a team of dedicated volunteers. The recruitment process includes:

- Developing a profile of the volunteers the organization needs.
- Developing a list of potential volunteers.
- Finding the right volunteer to make the "ask."
- Preparing a volunteer recruitment packet.
- Meeting face to face with prospective volunteers to invite their involvement.
- Welcoming and orienting the volunteers.
- Providing education and support for the volunteers.
- Managing the volunteer program.
- Appreciating and recognizing volunteers.

For organizations that have been using volunteers in areas such as program or administration, a good suggestion is to begin with those volunteers who have already demonstrated a commitment to the organization. Bring these volunteers together for a meeting to discuss fundraising roles. Another option is to survey current volunteers to see which ones have an interest in taking on new responsibilities in the form of fundraising opportunities. If the organization has used volunteers in minor fundraising roles such as helping at special events or stuffing envelopes, these volunteers should be asked if they have an interest in becoming involved at a deeper level such as requesting contributions.

For organizations that have never used volunteers, a good place to start is with those who have already shown an interest in the organization or have a tie to it. Alumni are found in many organizations, not just educational institutions. Perhaps the nonprofit has individuals who have participated in a rehabilitation program, taken an art class, or have been a blood donor. These are the organization's "alumni." Do not overlook them. They already know the organization and are often very committed to it.

There are other ways to attract fundraising volunteers. Local chambers of commerce are great ways to connect with businesspeople and entrepreneurs who are looking for opportunities to get more involved in their communities. Many communities also have leadership programs in which managers enroll in programs to learn more about the nonprofit world with the goal of serving on the board of a nonprofit organization. These programs can be a great source of volunteers. Nonprofit leaders need to become accustomed to the "rubber chicken circuit," speaking at meetings of local service and professional associations that might be able to volunteer as a group or individually. Many communities also have a volunteer center that matches volunteers with organizations and performs much of the screening of volunteers.

Past donors are an especially good source of volunteers. If they have already supported the organization, it will be easy for them to invite others to join them in this investment. A group of past donors could be invited to a special luncheon at which volunteer opportunities are presented.

Another way to find good volunteers is to involve staff and board members in the identification process. A process should be developed that enables the organization to establish volunteer needs and the qualities needed to fill each role. Have board and staff members brainstorm at a meeting to identify a list of potential volunteers who might have the qualities to fill these roles. Then develop a plan to select those who best meet the needs of the organization and begin to recruit them.

Sources of Volunteers

Where can volunteers be found to help with fundraising? Here are some sources:

- Donors.
- Other volunteers.
- Clients or users of services.
- Service clubs (Rotary, Lions, Sertoma, Kiwanis).
- Religious institutions.
- Chambers of commerce.
- Board members' suggestions.
- Fundraising committee suggestions.
- Website visitors.
- Leadership programs.
- Volunteer centers.
- Newsletter readers.
- Staff contacts.
- Businesses.
- Senior citizen centers.
- Universities.
- High schools.

Recruiting Volunteers

Here are some hints on recruiting from some of these groups:

- It is usually more effective to have a member of the organization ask for volunteers rather than an outsider.
- Most religious organizations have specific procedures for requesting volunteers. Begin by asking the religious leaders how to recruit volunteers from among their organization's members.

- Many businesses have a formal volunteer program. Ask for volunteers with specific types of expertise (for example, computer or public relations skills).

- Many senior centers are willing to recruit volunteers for you, especially if you make a donation to the center.

- Fraternities and sororities are excellent sources of volunteer help.

- Students studying a specific discipline (journalism or statistics, for example) may prove helpful.

- Many schools have formal internship programs.

- High school students might also be available to work at special events. Talk to the advisors in the school to see if there are groups such as a Key Club that might be available or if the school requires students to do community service.

Potential volunteers should be given a written position description with as detailed information as possible, including the following:

- Overall responsibilities.
- Specific tasks.
- Experience required.
- Supervision provided.
- Training provided.
- Time commitment.
- Flexibility of time required.
- Location of volunteer commitment.

Staff, board, or other volunteers can recruit volunteers. Getting the volunteers involved in finding individuals similar to themselves who share an interest in the mission of the organization is the best way to recruit.

Ways to Involve Volunteers

For many organizations, the annual fund involves direct mail, possibly a telephone campaign, and sometimes a corporate appeal.

The nonprofit that is successful in meeting the challenge of giving volunteers a meaningful and rewarding part in its development program is the one that involves volunteers in every aspect of its fundraising effort, starting with the annual fund. Having a volunteer chair or co-chair the annual fund can lend special credibility to the organization when approaching donors. The chair of the annual fund will guide the overall appeal, which might include a corporate appeal, a major gift effort, a phonathon, a direct mail campaign, and special events.

Involving Volunteers in the Direct Mail Appeal

Organizations can utilize volunteers to stuff mailings. Numerous groups such as senior or youth groups are happy for an activity that helps them meet their service requirements or fill time. But volunteers can also be used in other, more meaningful ways during a direct mail effort. Receiving a letter written by the parent of child killed by a drunk driver, a student on a scholarship, or a recovering addict is far more motivating to the potential donor than receiving a letter from the staff or board chair of the organization. Staff members should draft the letter for the volunteer, inviting their input to personalize it.

Another way to use volunteers effectively is to hold a focus group with potential donors and have attendees provide input into the direct mail package as it is being developed. Ask volunteers how they would respond to the carrier (outside) envelope, the letter, and any enclosures that may be included in the package. Volunteers can also be extremely helpful in expanding and correcting the mailing list.

Involving Volunteers in Telephone Fundraising

Volunteers are effective in a phonathon. It is important to remember, however, that phonathon volunteers must be carefully trained and provided with scripts and other materials they will need to be successful. Often, individuals identifying themselves as volunteers when calling are well-received because of their belief in the cause. Volunteers can also be invited to participate in thank-a-thons, in which volunteers will call donors to thank them for their gift, not to ask for money. This is an activity particularly suited to getting board members involved in the fundraising activities of the organization. When feasible, this is effectively done by recipients of the organization's services.

Involving Volunteers in a Business Appeal

Corporate and business appeals are far more effective when the business owner or manager is contacted by a peer volunteer. An annual corporate appeal, done through face-to-face, personal solicitations, has been tried by many nonprofits and found to be the most successful way to approach businesses. Volunteers enable an organization to reach many business leaders who have previously been impossible to meet. The volunteers are calling on someone with whom they have a personal and/or a business relationship.

Involving Volunteers in Special Events

Special events in almost every organization rely heavily on volunteers. Most special events are both staff- and volunteer-intensive. Volunteers usually serve in a variety of capacities on special event committees. As with any type of fundraising effort, leadership is critical to success. A special event committee chair can make or break the event.

Involving Volunteers in the Grants Process

Staff members usually prepare grant proposals except in very small organizations that have no staff. Volunteers might then step in to fill this role. However, proposals to foundations and corporations still need that personal touch. One way to give volunteers a meaningful part in grant fundraising is to review the list of potential funders with a committee and/or the board to determine where there may be personal contacts. A list should be developed showing the trustees of the foundations or corporate contacts. Asking volunteers to review this list and identify any trustees with whom they have a personal contact or companies they may do business with will help when developing a personalized appeal. Furthermore, volunteers should be invited to attend meetings with potential funders to help add credibility to the organization and speak to the funders from the point of view of a volunteer who has committed time and money to the organization.

Involving Volunteers in Soliciting Major Gifts

Although there are numerous roles volunteers can play in the annual fundraising program, perhaps none is more critical than the role of identifying, cultivating, and soliciting major donors. For many donors, the solicitor is one of the most important factors in determining the financial commitment they will make. Most individuals like to be asked by someone they know. A colleague or friend, sometimes even a relative, usually has much more success than a staff member.

Involving Volunteers in Planned Giving Efforts

Though planned giving is often thought of as a staff or consultant's role because of the specialized knowledge involved, volunteers can help in numerous ways. A committee of volunteer professional advisors can be effective in teaching the staff about various planned giving instruments, developing effective promotional materials for planned giving, making connections for the organization with potential donors, and conducting planned giving seminars.

Volunteers who have already made a planned gift themselves are the best spokespersons for the organization's planned giving program, and should be invited to help identify other potential donors and to introduce these donors to the organization. Volunteers can be asked to give testimonials or write an article for the organization's newsletter about why they made a planned gift to the organization.

The Fundraising Committee

The fundraising committee leads the organization's fundraising program. This committee, however, should not consist solely of board members. Involving volunteers on the committee not only helps the organization fulfill its fundraising goals but also provides a great training ground for prospective board members.

Finding members of committees is often easier than finding board members. Many individuals who may not be ready to accept the fiduciary responsibilities of a board member may want to get involved with the organization in other capacities. Some groups of individuals who may be potential fundraising committee members are bankers, financial planners, attorneys, media representatives, and entrepreneurs. Look for individuals who have served on boards or fundraising committees of other organizations.

Recruiting a development professional from another institution, providing that organization is not a direct competitor, may be helpful. Development professionals may choose not to help actively solicit donors because it could be a real or perceived conflict of interest. However, they may assist in planning, writing, or identifying donors. For example, a development officer from a university could be a good individual to add to the fundraising committee of a human service agency whose programs and donors will not be in competition with the university.

Ready to Go

If an agency makes maximum use of board members, staff members, and non-board volunteers in fundraising, it is well on its way to running a successful fundraising program.

Chapter 5
Looking for Grant Sources

Submitting proposals to government agencies, foundations, businesses, and individuals is an effective fundraising tool. The grants an agency receives are usually much larger than the amount of funds that would result from special events, direct mail, or a phonathon.

Look for information about grant sources in numerous locations. Some of these include online research tools, subscriptions to which can either be purchased by the organization or used for free at a local library. A tremendous amount of free information exists on the Internet using search engines such as Google, going to the Website of the funder, or searching *www.guidestar.org* or *www.grants.gov*. After weighing the costs and time involved for research, each organization must develop its own plan for researching various sources of grant funds concurrently.

Remember that diversification is a good strategy not only in the stock market but in the grants and fundraising area as well. If the organization receives grant funding from several businesses, foundations, government agencies, and individuals, it will be much easier to weather any storm that comes its way. It is often the case that obtaining a number of small grants may be easier than trying to land the big one.

One effective method to refine this preliminary research is to meet with individuals who either are representatives of funding sources or who can make referrals to representatives of funding sources.

Ask Political Representatives

An excellent source of grant information for national funding sources is through the two federal senators and local congressperson. State government grants are also available, so the organization should meet with state senators and representatives. Local municipalities such as cities and counties may also be a possibility, especially for "pass through" grants in which the local municipalities may award federal funds. Community Development Block Grants (CDBG) money, which flows from the federal government through counties and cities, is a good example of this type of funding source.

Begin the process by meeting with political representatives at the federal, state, and local levels. Do not wait to do this until the organization is asking for funds. Get to know political leaders, giving them information about legislation the organization supports or opposes. Meet their staff members in the local district on a personal basis. Ask for a meeting just to let them know the services the agency offers. In this way, they can refer potential clients when their constituents contact them. Give political leaders current and accurate information about the needs of the individuals the organization serves. Make sure to ask staff members of political leaders to contact the organization when they hear of a possible funding source. Although nonprofits can jeopardize their tax-exempt status by lobbying, asking legislators to notify nonprofits of grant opportunities is not considered a lobbying activity.

Political leaders can also help by writing letters of support to include with grant applications being submitted to funding sources. In many instances, a political leader can insert a funding request in a federal, state, or local budget. This process, called "earmarking," is often an effective way of obtaining funds without having to write a detailed funding application. Although this issue at times may become a political football, it is advisable to ask state and federal officials if earmarks are available.

In some instances, it may be helpful for a political leader to make a phone call or write a letter to encourage a government agency to fund an application that an organization has submitted. Be very careful when you do this, however. It may also work to the organization's disadvantage if the funding source resents political interference or dislikes the particular individual making the call.

Consider United Way

One important source of funding is United Way. The practices of United Ways differ widely, so check with the local United Way. There are more than 2,000 United Way agencies in the United States, and nearly every community in the country is represented by one. A general advantage of United Way funding is that many permit or even encourage continuous funding. Once the organization gets funded and continues to provide excellent service, it will more than likely receive funding in succeeding years.

One disadvantage of United Way funding is that they often place restrictions on other fundraising efforts. Some place restrictions only during the United Way campaign season or "blackout period." Others place restrictions year-round. Make sure to ask for and follow the United Way rules before applying for funding.

Foundation Proposals

Foundations are a major source of funding for nonprofits. When researching foundations, it becomes clear that there are many differences among the various types of foundations. Most private foundations are organizations that have been funded by wealthy individuals who often have a specific type of nonprofit organization they tend to support. Some foundations are started by businesses as a vehicle to provide charitable donations rather than give from their corporate account.

Many foundations are started by individuals under provisions established in their wills. These foundations are often managed by family members and are rather informal. Still other foundations are community foundations that have been established to raise money from donors and disperse them to community groups. Other foundations, known as operating foundations, are set up to fund a specific nonprofit or a specific area such as research and do not accept applications for funding.

The first step when researching a foundation is to find out as much as you can, for example:

- From where does it receive its funds?
- What types of organizations does it fund?
- How much does it disperse annually?
- What is the typical grant size?
- Does it fund operating costs, capital campaigns, or endowments?

Usually this information is available on the foundation's Website. Some smaller foundations may not have a Website, but most foundations have annual reports. All foundations are required to fill out a report annually with the Internal Revenue Service (990 PF). That information is public knowledge and can be found on *www.guidestar.org*. Large foundations have staff, and a letter or phone call will get the information you need.

It is essential to learn what types of organizations the foundation funds. Legal precedents are clear that, with few exceptions, the trustees of a private foundation cannot change the wishes of the donor as to what the foundation can fund. However, corporate and community foundations often change their priorities, so it is important to keep abreast of their current guidelines and interests.

New needs may arise in a community, and most foundations will attempt to address these needs when establishing grant priorities.

A good place to research foundations is the local library. Some libraries have been designated as Foundation Center Cooperating Libraries. The Foundation Center is an organization that collects information about foundations and sells it to potential users. These grant center libraries have special materials for grant seekers, both online and in print. Other sources that have this information are found at *www.bigonlinedatabase.com* and *www.grantstation.com*. However, all of these sources require fees to use their services unless you can access them at the local library.

Research every foundation carefully before asking for a meeting with foundation representatives or applying for funds. Learn the following:

- Type of programs the foundation funds.
- Size and purpose of grants awarded.
- Application information required.
- Application deadlines.
- Guidelines as to types of funding they provide (annual, capital, endowment, and so on).
- Types of organizations they fund (arts, healthcare, education, and so on).

Try to arrange a meeting with a representative of the foundation to obtain information about the grants it provides. The first choice would be to meet with the foundation donor (or with family members if the donor is deceased). Larger foundations have program officers, some of whom may focus on specific areas, such as education, health, or the arts. All foundations have trustees. However, small, private foundations may not have staff or even an office, and often the trustees meet sporadically when there are proposals to be considered. Larger foundations will have more formalized procedures and may ask you to deal only with a program officer.

Service Groups

Every community has a large number of professional and service groups, some connected with religious institutions, that raise funds for nonprofit organizations. It is always helpful when the request for funds comes from an individual who is a member of that group rather than an outsider. Often a helpful process is to ask board members, volunteers, and other constituents to which groups they belong.

Before submitting a proposal to any service group, it is important to research the past giving of the groups. How much did they raise in the past? What are the restrictions under which they operate? What is their area of interest? For example, Lions Clubs often support the visually impaired, whereas Sertoma chapters help the hearing impaired. Many other groups have their own particular areas of interest. Even if the organization does not fit into their primary area of interest, some service groups may still fund a project because it helps the local community.

Many service groups have regular meetings and would be pleased to invite a representative of the organization to speak about the group's activities. Some "adopt" nonprofit groups and help them in fundraising efforts. Some service groups will operate their own programs and then donate the funds to nonprofit organizations.

Submitting Proposals to Corporate Foundations

It is rare that a nonprofit agency receives a grant from a business or corporate foundation without meeting first with representatives of the funding source or contacting them by phone or e-mail. Chapter 7 in this book (Raising Money From Businesses) includes a description of how to form relationships with the local business community. Once staff members or volunteers of the organization get to know business leaders personally, it will be easy to ask if there is a corporate foundation and what its funding policies are. If there is no corporate foundation, ask to meet personally with representatives of the business.

If there is a foundation, researching it is critical. Some corporate foundations have detailed requests for proposals that are very similar to those of private foundations. Others will just request a letter stating what the organization will be doing with the funds and how much is being requested. Keep in mind that often a local branch of a company can be helpful in submitting a request to its corporate foundation. Often these foundations, however, are more interested in national or international projects and may not be as supportive of local efforts as the local branch would be.

Always ask for as much information as possible about the corporate foundation's procedures. Sometimes, the company's annual report will provide useful information. Some companies have a staff person, a community relations department, or a contributions committee. A meeting with that individual or group is always useful. Also, some corporations have policies that state that they only give to organizations in which their employees are involved. When this is the case, getting some of the company's employees involved as volunteers is essential. Other corporations only give grants to organizations located in communities where they have corporate branches.

Submitting Proposals to Government Agencies

A great deal of information can be found online about government grant opportunities. The easiest tool to use is *www.grants.gov.* Many organizations that are successful in obtaining federal grants deal directly with the offices in Washington, D.C., and the applications are all prepared online. Once on the grants.gov Website, seek out the various departments that fund projects that might benefit specific organizations or programs, such as the Department of Justice, Department of Health and Human Services, National Endowment for the Arts (NEA), or National Endowment for Humanities (NEH). Once an organization has been funded by the federal government, it will likely receive notices of additional funding that becomes available.

Begin the process of applying to government agencies by forming relationships with staff members of the government agency that gives grants. Staff of a health clinic, for example, should meet with representatives of the state Department of Health. An arts group would meet with a staff member of the state's arts council. In many instances, federal agencies have branch offices in the state. An organization involved in the housing field, for example, should take the time to meet with the local HUD representative. The U.S. Department of Agriculture funds a wide range of programs for rural areas, and has numerous offices in local areas throughout the country. Ask for a meeting with a local USDA staffer and ask about available programs.

Once the government agency that gives grants is located, ask for a meeting with a representative of that agency. Ask for copies of proposals it has funded in the past. Because the agency has spent public dollars, more information about past grants is available than from private businesses.

Submitting Proposals to Individuals

Many individuals are more receptive to funding specific proposals than just writing a check to the agency. In many instances, it is possible to get a multi-year commitment from individuals. Meet with potential funders first. When they declare their interests, a proposal should then be submitted to them consistent with these interests.

Chapter 6
Writing Proposals and Getting Them Funded

Grant research is very time consuming. In addition, the time spent in writing the grant proposal may be extensive. So how does the small organization accomplish all of this?

One suggestion is to begin by carefully planning what type of grants the agency will be seeking. Every funding source—whether government, foundation, or business, large or small—asks basically the same questions. So begin by collecting answers to these standard questions. Then it will be fairly easy to develop a generic grant proposal. Of course, each proposal will need to be customized to fit the interests and requirements of each funder. However, having a generic grant already prepared will save a great deal of time when a grant opportunity presents itself.

Arrange all the information listed here in a computer with appropriate backup. This is called the "grants vault." Then when a possible funding source is located, ask for the funder's instructions, often called a request for proposal, or RFP. Select the information from the vault that will be needed to prepare the grant application. Often, the funding source asks for a letter outlining the request, usually called a Letter of Inquiry. If the funder is interested in the project, it will then invite the organization to submit a formal grant proposal. Most often, the funding source will request specific forms to be attached to the grant request, and the information to complete these forms will also be available from the vault. Copies of the organization's IRS designation letter as a 501 (c)(3) tax-exempt organization will almost always be requested.

Here are some of the common questions asked by funders:

Need

What are the needs of the individuals in the community for the services the grant would provide? Some requests for proposal ask for a statement of the problem. Remember that the agency is being asked for the need of the potential clients for the service—not the need of the agency for the funds. Also, it will be much more effective to state the needs in statistical or numerical form rather than as a narrative.

Here are some ways to quantify the need:

- **Survey:** Ask an individual with expertise in this field, perhaps a statistics teacher or a college intern, to show the staff how to conduct a survey to find out the need for a particular program or service. Once the survey instrument is developed, staff members or volunteers may be able to ask the necessary questions and tabulate the data. A college statistics class could undertake the survey as a class project. There are also online tools available, such as Survey Monkey, which can facilitate the process of completing the questionnaires and tabulating results.

- **Ask present clients:** Sit down with present clients and discuss with them the need for a particular service for which the agency is requesting funds. If 80 percent of clients say they would use a new service, this would be an effective statement of need. This can be done in a group setting or one on one.

- **Waiting lists or letters requesting a service:** Be sure to maintain records of individuals requesting services not currently offered.

- **Public meeting:** Many organizations have been successful in calling a public meeting and taking testimony on the need for a particular service.

- **Census data:** Often, information from the census provides the best statistical data for the need for a particular program. For example, housing and homelessness data are available through the census.

- **Governmental data:** State departments of health should be approached to obtain health data; the Office of Employment Security will provide the latest employment information; local police departments are an excellent source of crime statistics.

Objectives

The funder will ask for proposed objectives. Sometimes funders will ask for goals or proposed accomplishments.

Objectives have five characteristics, as already discussed in Chapter 1. These characteristics are often referred to as SMART objectives:

- **Specific:** The objectives should list specific tasks to be accomplished, such as "We will feed 2,000 children a nutritious meal."

- **Measurable:** Estimate how many clients will be served, how many jobs will be obtained, or any other objective in specific numbers. Before listing an objective in the proposal, think through whether it can be measured if the proposal is funded.

- **Action-oriented:** The objective must outline specific steps to be taken. For example, provide an objective such as "Print and distribute 2,500 copies of an informational piece about the dangers of smoking in 15 high schools," rather than a nebulous idea like increasing awareness of the dangers of smoking to teens.

- **Realistic:** Resist the urge to make up large numbers that cannot be achieved. Remember that, if the proposal gets funded, the organization will often be asked to sign a contract that obligates it to meet these objectives.

- **Time-defined:** Set objectives for a specific time period such as year, a quarter, or a month.

Examples of objectives might be:

- Obtaining full-time employment for 100 program participants during the funding year.

- Attendance of 250 individuals in a training program.

- Reduction in drug use by 20 percent of the program participants within three months of participating in the program.

Activities

The proposal should always give a description of the services to be provided if the funds are awarded. Always be as clear as possible, because often the individual reading the proposal is not familiar with the services provided. Try to avoid agency or industry jargon. When using an abbreviation or acronym, indicate what the letters stand for.

Activity schedules, procedure manuals, lesson plans, and descriptions of equipment are all helpful in outlining the use of the funds requested. It may be helpful to have a draft of this section read by an individual who does not work in the agency. Ask this person if he or she understands what services you are providing.

The six "W" questions must be answered:

- **Who?** Who are the participants and how are they selected for participation in the program? Are there restrictions (for example, age, income, residence location)? Who are the staff members and what are their credentials?
- **What?** Exactly what services will be provided?
- **Where?** Where will the services be provided? At multiple locations, in the schools, in the home of the recipients, at a senior center?
- **When?** What are the hours, days, and times of the year when services will be provided?
- **With whom?** Be as specific as possible about the other agencies with whom the nonprofit will be collaborating. Explain the services each one provides the clients and how this relates to the services being funded by this proposal.
- **Why?** What is the uniqueness of this program? Why is the organization providing these services rather than other services?

Job Descriptions

Make certain to include job descriptions for each individual being paid with grant funds. List the tasks the individual would be performing in priority order. Outline the credentials these staff people have for providing services. List a salary for each individual that is consistent with the salary figure in the budget. Do not forget fringe benefits and taxes when preparing a budget.

Evaluation

Most funding sources will ask how the results of the program will be evaluated. Think this through carefully before replying. Possible questions to consider may include the following:

- **Who will participate?** Outline how board members, staff members, and clients will participate in the evaluation.
- **What will be the evaluation tools?** If a training program is provided, include the test that will be given to the attendees. If all program participants will be interviewed as part of the evaluation process, include the interview form. If an evaluation committee will be formed, indicate who will serve on this committee.
- **What will be evaluated?** Try to anticipate some of the evaluation questions. A client satisfaction survey may be helpful, for example.

Check attendance figures to see if attendance objectives were met. If there was a waiting list for a particular program, see if those on the list are now participating in the program. Measurable outcomes are a critical requirement of most funders.

Budget

It is important for the agency and the funding source that an accurate estimate of budget expenditures be provided. When requesting a grant to purchase equipment, obtain cost estimates for that equipment before submitting the proposal. If requesting funds to hire staff, determine the salary for the staff member and compute the fringe benefits before submitting the proposal. These costs should be in line with costs for similar agencies in the community.

Read the instructions carefully. The funder will always ask for the amount of funds being requested, though the question will be asked in different ways. Some simply ask for the total amount of money being requested. Many times an RFP includes specific budget categories, and it is critical to carefully estimate expenses in each category. The funder may also ask what other sources of funding are anticipated to share the costs of this program. This may include other grants that are anticipated, program revenue, or money from the agency's operating budget. Many funders do not want to be the only source of funding for any project. All are interested in a viable plan for continuing the project at the end of the funding period.

Some funding sources request a line item budget. The organization will be required to estimate each expense, each salary, and every piece of equipment. Some grants require "matching funds." The request for proposal will outline this if it is required. Ask if "in-kind" (non-cash) contributions can be provided or if a cash match will be required. If in-kind funds are acceptable, begin with volunteer time. Estimate the number of hours that will be volunteered during the grant period. Volunteer time should be valued at the market rate for the services. If an attorney is providing legal advice pro bono, for example, his or her rate would be the rate the attorney charges paying clients. Include the market value of computers, duplicating machines, and other donated items. The Internal Revenue Service can provide guidelines on valuing the services of volunteers.

Letters of Support

When applying for most grants, the decision as to whether to include letters of support is one that must be made. Sometimes the funder will specify a maximum number of letters of support to be included. The RFP is often silent on this issue. As with most decisions, it is based on a tradeoff between the time it takes to get the letters and the likelihood they will help in being awarded the grant. Getting the advice of a representative of the funding source may be helpful in making the decision. If letters of support will be included, have them addressed to the organization and include them in the proposal rather than asking the writer to send them directly to the funding source.

There are three types of letters of support:

- **Letters from potential or existing clients:** A letter from a client outlining the need for the specific service for which the request is being made can be very powerful. When seeking funds to expand an existing service, letters from present clients stating specifically how they have been helped by the service should be included with the proposal.

- **Letters from cooperating agencies:** Include letters from the executive director of agencies with whom the organization collaborates on a regular basis. Ask the writers to be as specific as possible. Suggest that they include examples of how funding this program will help them serve their clients.

- **Letters from political leaders:** Letters from the state's two senators and congressperson, the state senator or representative, county officials, and the mayor of the town or city in which the organization is located can be helpful. Ask these individuals to be as specific as possible as to how the grant would help their constituents. Often, giving these political leaders "talking points" outlining suggestions as to what to include in the letter may be helpful.

Funding Strategies

When the request for proposal is obtained from the funding source, it must be read very carefully. Follow the instructions meticulously. If the organization would like to deviate from the instructions, contact a representative of the funding source and obtain written permission to do so. Funding sources like to see organizations cooperating in the submission of a proposal. Chances of funding are increased if several agencies with a joint mission apply for funds.

Meeting with a representative of the funding source is a good idea. Ask for the meeting in each case. Before this meeting, write as much of the grant as possible so questions are as specific as possible. If the request for a meeting is denied, try a phone call, e-mail, or letter to get answers to the following questions before writing the proposal:

- **How much money is being given out in grants?** Most governmental agencies will provide this figure. Obviously, the chances to get a grant are different if the agency is giving out a million dollars than if it is awarding a hundred million.

- **Will the funder provide copies of grants that were funded in previous years?** This would help greatly in the grant quest. Many government agencies and foundations will provide a list of the amount of past grants and the name and address of the agency receiving them. Each grant recipient can then be contacted and asked for a copy of the grant. Just knowing the kind of agencies funded in the past and the amount of the grants will help in deciding whether to apply and how much to request.

- **How long should the application be?** In most cases, there is a limited amount of available time to write the proposal, so each one should be as short as possible. On the other hand, the application may not be funded because it is too short. Also be aware that more and more proposals, especially from government agencies, require online submission. There may be strict guidelines about how lengthy the application can be.

- **What are the procedures regarding online applications?** Every funder is different. Many now require that all proposals be submitted online, and others require hard-copy submission. Still others leave the decision to the applicant.

- **How much should the organization apply for?** This is a critical question to ask. In many situations, the needs of the clients are limitless. If the funding source would grant a million dollars, most agencies could put it to good use. Some funders will not fund an organization that asks for too much. Others may fund an amount less than requested. On the other hand, some funders think on a much larger scale and may reject an application that they consider to be too small. It is critical to check the typical grant amounts of the funder before applying.

- **What are the chances for renewed or multi-year funding?** Often a grant is given for a one-year period, but it is renewable. Ask this question before applying. If there is a possibility of renewing the grant, find out when the application for second-year funding is due. When hiring a staff person with grant funds, prepare a plan for continuing the individual's salary after the grant ends. If applying for a one-year grant, think carefully how the organization will pay staff costs and other expenditures at the end of the year. If there is no alternate source of funding, it may be wise not to apply for a one-year grant. If renewed funding is anticipated, the organization will make different decisions than if the funding source states that this is a non-renewable grant. The funder may also ask how the agency will continue the program once the grant cycle has ended, so the nonprofit must be prepared to show a long-term plan for financing this program. When applying for a grant to purchase a piece of equipment, a single-year grant is acceptable.

- **Who makes the funding decisions, and what are their backgrounds?** If those making the funding decisions are experts in the field, the application will be written much differently than if they have no knowledge of the industry.

- **How many other agencies are applying for these grants?** Knowing who the competition is can be very helpful, especially if the grants are limited.

Before You Submit the Proposal

Before mailing the proposal, read it one more time. Make certain the application is completely filled out. Answer every question. Follow every instruction.

Are all of the funder's questions answered? Is every word spelled correctly? Is it interesting to read? If you were the grantor, would you fund it?

Chapter 7
Raising Money From Businesses

There is a saying in fundraising: "If you want advice, ask for money; if you want money, ask for advice." This adage is especially true when it comes to raising funds from the local business community. Many nonprofit organizations cannot seem to figure out why their local business communities are not supporting them financially. There may be several answers to this question:

- The organization does not understand that companies are in business to make a profit, not to be philanthropic.
- The organization has not built relationships with individuals in the business community.
- The organization has not stressed the advantage to the business of making a contribution.
- The organization used a direct mail program to approach businesses rather than visiting businesses individually.

Some large nonprofit organizations such as universities lump businesses with foundations and set up a corporate and foundation gifts department within their development offices. The two entities are very different and, therefore, the approaches to them must be very different. Foundations are in business to give away money, whereas corporations are in business to make money for their stockholders. It is as simple as that! Even a small business owner who may not have stockholders has set up the business with the goal of showing a profit. This is sometimes a simple concept that nonprofits find hard to grasp, particularly if most of their previous fundraising efforts have been focused on government or foundation grants.

Does this mean that businesses and corporations are uncharitable or selfish? No. They are a viable part of every community, creating jobs, bringing tourists or other businesses into the community, and generating tax revenues. Remember that most individuals, including business owners, care very deeply about their communities. Many businesses are socially conscious, and even those that are not as altruistic will often give to nonprofits because of the direct or indirect benefit to their company or their employees.

So, how can an organization know what motivates its local businesses to give to charitable causes? Ask them! Asking for the advice of local business leaders before asking for money is one of the keys to success. And, as in all fundraising, corporate and business fundraising is built on the three key words in fundraising: relationships, relationships, relationships.

Begin by identifying businesses in the community to ask for funds. Here are a few examples:

- Chamber of commerce members.
- Vendors from whom the agency purchases goods and services.
- Employers of board members and spouses of staff members.
- Companies that have given to other nonprofits.
- Companies that have an affiliation to or an interest in the services the nonprofit provides.

The local chamber of commerce can be very helpful in identifying local businesses. Becoming active in the chamber is a great way to build relationships with the business community. Likewise, local service clubs such as Rotary or Kiwanis can locate local business owners who can be involved in the organization and asked for funds.

The best way to obtain funding from a business that might assist the organization is to begin by informing the businessperson about the services of the agency. This can be done in many ways, such as:

- Inviting the businessperson to serve on a business advisory committee.
- Sending information about the agency on a regular basis.
- Inviting the businessperson to an open house.
- Visiting the business to find out what type of goods and services it offers.
- Inviting the businessperson to the agency for a meeting with the staff and a tour.

One great way to involve local business leaders is to invite them to attend a focus group session in which you provide information about the organization and then ask for their input. The key to successful business gatherings of this type is the invitation process. Ask a prominent local business leader with whom the organization already has an established relationship to invite some of his or her peers to attend a brief meeting. Provide a list of business leaders to involve and ask for additions. Often breakfast meetings are best for businesspeople so they can arrive early (perhaps 7:00 a.m. or 7:30 a.m.) and still get to their places of business by 8:30 a.m. or 9:00 a.m.

Do not have the meeting run more than an hour and a quarter. Inviting about 25 to 30 individuals will usually result in attendance of about a dozen or so businesspeople. If possible, take them for a brief tour of the facility or a virtual tour by video or Microsoft PowerPoint. Have a current client talk about the organization and

In order to determine how many volunteers you need, first make a list of all the companies in the community you would like to ask for a contribution. Then divide that list by five. Start small! You may have hundreds of businesses in the community, but select the ones with whom you think you will have the best chance of being successful. Select companies whose products are used by the clients, the organization's vendors, and companies that have employees that are involved in or connected to the organization. For example, maybe one or more of the local banks had teams in a golf tournament or bowl-a-thon. Certainly include the bank with which the agency does business. A healthcare facility should visit a local manufacturer of medical supplies or pharmaceuticals.

Ask the staff and board members for a list of companies with whom they do business or where they or their spouses work. Include the retail stores where clients and staff members shop. Select businesses with a track record of contributing to nonprofits. Groups in the community such as the symphony, hospital, United Way, and university alumni associations regularly publish lists of donors.

Chances for success increase dramatically if the company already knows about the organization. This is the time to approach those businesses who attended the advice-giving focus groups. From this list of potential donors, identify potential volunteers. Remember that many businesses only support nonprofits with which their employees are involved, so selecting the right volunteers is the key to the process. The more volunteers, the more companies can be approached. Once the program expands to what may seem an unmanageable size, divide the volunteers into teams of five people and work with team leaders.

Provide the volunteers with information about the organization that they can give to prospective donors. But remember: These are businesspeople, not foundation officers. They do not have the time, or perhaps even the interest, to read volumes of materials. A simple one-page fact sheet can be very helpful. Give the volunteers additional information such as brochures or annual reports for those prospects who request more detailed information.

A simple but professional-looking annual report is a great tool to which businesspeople can relate. Focus the appeal on a specific project or program such as a scholarship program for individuals who cannot afford the services. The materials should clearly make a compelling case why the local business community should support this program or project. Remember that a top-notch Website is essential. Many businesspeople would rather search the Website than read printed materials.

Be as specific as possible about why giving to the agency will help that business. Here are some tips:

- Learn the federal and state tax advantages for businesses giving to the agency.

- Stress that by helping the clients more individuals will have the funds to buy the products the business sells.

- Indicate how lowering crime and increasing education (or whatever service the organization provides) helps the entire community.

- Inform the business about how its contribution will be publicized, thus leading to good will for that business in the community.

- Make the point that a strong community will result in the ability for the business to recruit more qualified employees to work and live in that community.

The volunteers will need a training session in which they will learn how to make the case for the organization and how to ask for a gift. If this is the first time these volunteers have been involved with an appeal of this type, they may need more intense training on topics such as how to schedule a meeting. However, if the volunteers are fairly sophisticated and will be calling on their friends and peers, they may not need as much training.

Always begin with a kickoff meeting in which volunteers are given their information packets, receive training or a refresher in making the "ask," and any questions about the program are answered. Report meetings will also be important so volunteers can celebrate success, provide feedback on how the program is going, and receive hints from other volunteers on how to approach their prospects. Include an inspirational talk, such as from a client who is receiving services. At the end of the appeal, plan a victory celebration. Prizes can be given to the volunteers who have raised the most money or completed the most calls. Volunteers from the business community often are inspired by friendly competition. A staff person, board member, or volunteer might want to take on the challenge of soliciting some local restaurants and other businesses for gift certificates, which can be used as prizes. Keep all meetings short and at a convenient time for businesspeople, which often is the first thing in the morning.

All this takes time. Cultivating, researching, and finding the right volunteers are critical components of all fundraising. A corporate appeal is no different. Is it worth the time and effort? Yes. Having the local business community members as allies in the search for funds will be a major step in making corporate and business fundraising successful.

Chapter 8
Major Gifts

The key to a solid fundraising program is the major gifts program that focuses on the 5 to 10 percent of the organization's donors that usually provide 90 to 95 percent of the funds received by the organization. But how does the organization find and reach those donors? It comes about through the development of relationships with the organization. The board, staff, and volunteers of the organization must focus their energies on building lasting relationships with major donor prospects. That is why the fundraising process is called "development."

There are several steps to raising major gifts:

- Identifying major donor prospects.
- Cultivating these prospects.
- Recruiting the major gifts team.
- Training the team.

- Scheduling the appointments.
- Visiting the prospects.
- Asking for the gift.

Identifying Major Donor Prospects

Many times in smaller organizations, executive directors and development directors will bemoan the fact that they do not have the "movers and shakers" on their board and, therefore, cannot consider a major gift program. Before giving up, consider brainstorming major donor prospects. You may be surprised at the connections the board has in this regard.

Brainstorming is best done by a screening process conducted by the major gifts subcommittee, which is a subdivision of the fundraising committee. It is critical to get the right individuals on this subcommittee. Members of the fundraising committee who are focused on special events or grants will most likely not be the right people for this special task. The major gifts subcommittee should include:

- Board members.
- Staff members.
- Fundraising committee members.
- Volunteers with broad community connections.

Select subcommittee members very carefully and make them aware that the information shared in these meetings is confidential. If the board or committee volunteers have never done rating and screening before, explain to them that this method—Linkages, Ability, and Interest (the LAI Principle)—is used routinely in most organizations and is the best way to determine the key ingredients of a major gift. It is important the meeting that is led by an experienced group facilitator. The leader must keep the group on task and explain the methodology to those who are not familiar with the process.

It is important to start with a preliminary list, as it is often hard to get a brainstorming session started with a blank slate. Ask the staff to prepare a list of major donors to the organization or other prospects that may have the potential to make a major gift. Check with other organizations in the community including arts organizations, hospitals, schools, and United Ways. Pick up annual reports of other organizations, particularly those that might have a similar mission. They often list their major donors. See if any of these donors have a connection to your organization

Have the giving history of major donors to the organization available, including their largest gift and most recent gift. Provide a column for each of the key ingredients: Linkages, Ability, and Interest. Be sure to mark the sheets "Highly Confidential." Make sure to list the contacts of each individual with the organization. Do they receive the organization's newsletter, have they attended any programs, and have they ever served on the board or any committees?

Invite the group to assemble in a quiet room and open the discussion with a brief explanation of the process and its importance to the organization. Then distribute the lists prepared by the staff. Discuss each name, attempting to determine the best **Linkages**—who knows this individual best or would be the best person to make the "ask"? Often there will be several linkages, and the task of this group is to determine the best solicitation team.

Next, try to determine **Ability**—how large a gift could this individual give to the organization if so motivated? Without revealing confidential information, the subcommittee members often can estimate the prospect's net worth and income. Then try to determine **Interest**—does this individual have knowledge of the organization? Is this a cause he or she is known to support? Is there a specific program of the organization or part of the project that would especially interest this donor?

As each name is discussed, complete the form with the Linkages, Ability, and Interest outlined.

Although there are several other ways to build a list, the advantage of this method is that there is discussion and consensus. Be sure to encourage subcommittee members to add their own names to the list. Often, seeing the list will jog individuals to think of other potential donors for the organization. Planning and conducting a screening session may seem like quite an effort, but it will most likely uncover some hidden stars among current donors and uncover new prospects along the way.

Cultivating Donors

It is important to remember that volunteers should not expect to raise major gifts from those who are not familiar with both the organization and the volunteer inviting them to invest in the organization. In some cases, it may take months or even years to cultivate a prospective donor before asking for a major gift. Numerous cultivation activities and events are addressed in other chapters of this book, including holding a fundraising dinner (see Chapter 12) or an open house (see Chapter 13). Some donors may already be familiar with and supportive of the organization and will not need much cultivation. For those less familiar with the organization, it may take an extensive amount of time and effort to solidify the relationship with a prospective donor enough to invite them to make a major investment.

Building the Team

Major gifts are not the responsibility of one individual in any organization, but rather a team effort. The chief executive officer (executive director, pastor, president) plays a key role in the major gift process. Visionary and ethical leadership is one of the primary elements a major donor will consider before making a major investment in the organization. If the organization has a development officer, that individual will usually play a pivotal role in planning and organizing the major gift program as well as managing the time of staff and volunteers. Make certain to plan so there is sufficient time and training available for both staff and volunteers to build those critical relationships with major donors.

Board members and other volunteers are the most important parts of the team. Volunteers bring a special ability to open doors and speak peer-to-peer to potential major donors. They can talk with the enthusiasm of a donor who invites a friend or colleague to join in investing in an organization for which they have a shared passion. Although a staff member may be a member of the solicitation team, the volunteer spirit is so important that a volunteer should always be included.

It has been said that the key to a successful gift is having the right person ask the right person, at the right time, in the right way, for the right amount, and for the right reason. Finding the right person to make the "ask" is critical. During the screening and rating sessions, it will be essential to find the best asker. Several individuals might know the prospective donor, so the subcommittee must identify the individual with the best connection to the prospect.

The ability of the prospect to make a large gift must also be considered in order to make sure the ask amount is right. Research into past giving history, the prospect's history of giving to other organizations, and an estimate of the prospect's assets will help determine the ask amount. Staff can do some of this research, but much of the information is gathered during the screening and rating sessions.

In addition to information on past giving, it is helpful to have additional information about the prospective donor before setting up the appointment for the visit. The major gifts subcommittee should try to obtain the following information about each major gift prospect, remembering that, if the prospect is a couple, the information should be collected about both individuals:

- Profession.
- Marital status.
- Religious affiliation.
- Alma mater.

- Children/grandchildren.
- Hobbies.
- Awards.
- Openness to being approached.
- Interest in any particular program or aspect of the organization.
- Giving history.

The interest of the prospect should always be considered, particularly when the individual is a major donor prospect. Is there a named gift opportunity that fits this prospect's interest? Named gifts are opportunities for major donors to name a building, a room, or a piece of equipment after themselves, their family, their company, or a loved one.

Timing is also important. During the screening process, it should be determined whether the prospect is ready to be solicited or if more cultivation is needed before visiting a prospective donor. Remember that gifts should always be solicited with the donor's interests and needs in mind.

The volunteers who will be directly involved in soliciting donors will need to be trained in how best to make the "ask." Staff, volunteers, or a consultant can lead the training session. Keep in mind that the trainer must be skilled at helping volunteers develop an approach that uses their own unique style to present the case. Role-playing is often used during this training, and the trainer must be skilled in facilitating this role-playing.

Some of the key points to be covered with volunteers during the training sessions are:

- Solicitors must make their own gift first.
- Knowing about the agency and being able to talk passionately about it are critical.
- Two-person team solicitations are often the best approach for major gifts.

- The team needs to rehearse their approach beforehand, including determining which one will make the "ask."

- Getting the appointment is sometimes the hardest part of the call, so the individual who has the best contact with the prospect should schedule the appointment.

- When scheduling an appointment with a couple, make sure both are available for the meeting.

- Begin by stating briefly the mission of the organization.

- Ask the prospects to talk about their involvement with the agency.

- Ask the prospects to talk about anything that interests them (for example, children, grandchildren, hobbies).

- Thank the prospects for their past support of the community and the organization.

- The team should present the case using the materials that have been developed, speak with enthusiasm about the organization and its needs, and tell the prospects about how this project meets their interest.

- The solicitors must be prepared to demonstrate their own financial commitment.

- When it is determined that the time is right, one of the solicitors will make the "ask."

- Always ask for a specific amount—the amount that has been determined in advance of the visit.

- The amount of the request is the largest amount you think the prospects may give.

- The way the "ask" is phrased is important. Use words or phrases such as *investment* or *joining us in the vision*, rather than asking for a donation or contribution.

- Once the "ask" is made, the solicitors should remain silent and wait for the prospects to react.

- The solicitors should be prepared to answer any questions the prospects have or be willing to get the answers to those questions.

- If the prospects say no, the solicitors should probe for the reasons. Is it "no, not that amount," "no, not now," or "no, not for that project"?

- Once the prospects have indicated the amount of the gift, the solicitor should have them fill out a pledge card.

- Solicitors should not leave a pledge card for the prospects to return by mail, because this usually results in a lower gift or no gift at all.

- If prospects do not wish to make a pledge on the spot but wish to think about it or discuss with their spouse/partner and/or financial advisors, the solicitor should set a specific time to make a return visit or call on the phone to obtain a pledge.

- All visits should end with the solicitor thanking the prospects for their time and interest.

- Follow-up is vital to success, so a thank-you note should be sent along with any information the prospects have requested.

Making the "Ask"

Volunteers must realize that they are not begging for money but are giving individuals an opportunity to be a part of the exciting work of the organization. Major gift team members need to understand that giving really does feel good and that being generous even makes individuals live longer! Team members need to experience the joy of giving themselves. One of the keys to a successful solicitation is that all askers must make their own gift first. It is a proven fact that those who have made a gift will always be more successful at asking others to give, because they can ask the prospect to "join me in investing in this great project." Of course the team members also need to be convinced that what they are asking for is a worthy project; the organization must have a compelling case for support.

Through the screening process, board members and other volunteers will have identified individuals with whom they have a relationship and feel comfortable asking. In most cases, the asker should be giving at a level equal to what he or she is asking others to give. It is usually easier for individuals to ask someone they know than a total stranger. It all goes back to the compelling case: If volunteers really believe in the mission of the organization and know others who share their values and beliefs, it is very likely that their friends will also be interested in supporting this organization. Always have volunteers start with a visit that is likely to be successful. Nothing builds enthusiasm the way success does. A volunteer who has made that first successful call will be far more motivated to continue making calls.

In summary, the steps to a successful "ask" are:

- Ask a peer.
- Know the "case."
- Be sure the solicitor makes his or her own gift first.
- Know the donor's needs and interests.
- Ask for a specific amount.
- Ask for enough.
- Plan the next step.

The 5-Call Rule

It is important not to ask too much of board members and volunteers, especially the first time around. No team member should be asked to make more than about five personal visits. That is usually a manageable number for most solicitors. Give the volunteer fundraisers any information that will be helpful in their call. Include the donor's past giving history to the organization, if any, other gifts that this individual may have made in the community (a little research will help build the chances for a successful call), and any connection this prospective donor has to the organization.

Bring in someone to train the team in how to make the "ask." The training should include having them always ask for a specific amount for a specific project. And remember that individuals are usually not insulted by being asked for too much, but they can be insulted by being asked for too little!

Team Spirit and Motivation

Make sure to schedule regular reporting meetings so team members can share successes and challenges they have faced. Knowing others are sharing their experiences helps build a team spirit and helps volunteers solve some of the challenges they may be having. Everyone likes to report their successes. Often the volunteers have a healthy sense of competition once they get going. Having an opportunity to report their success to others is often a strong motivator. This meeting will help build enthusiasm and help plan for the next approach to each prospective donor. A few large gifts will be the motivator needed to make all the other parts of the fundraising campaign successful.

Always be encouraging. Remember that, especially if this is a first major gift effort for the organization, not all calls are going to be successful. Encourage volunteers to continue by stressing that they are building relationships and not just raising money. After all, the three keys to successful fundraising are relationships, relationships, relationships.

Chapter 9
Direct Mail

Direct mail is one form of fundraising that almost any organization can accomplish with relative ease. It is the type of fundraising that allows the organization to reach the most individuals.

Several types of direct mail play an important role in the overall fundraising program, such as:

- Acquisition mailings.
- Renewal mailings.
- Cultivation mailings.
- Acknowledgment mailings.

What Are Acquisition Mailings and How Are They Used?

The term *acquisition mailing* is used to describe a mailing made by an organization that does not already have a built-in base of constituents who could be likely supporters of their fundraising efforts. Some organizations may never use acquisition mailing. A college or university, for example, seldom does acquisition mailing because they have a donor base of alumni. Hospitals, likewise, usually have a significant number of "grateful patients" to solicit, so they may not need to conduct acquisition mailings. Religious organizations are also unlikely to use acquisition mailings unless they are attempting to reach out to their community for more members.

On the other hand, a local homeless shelter, domestic violence group, or other human service organization often does acquisition mailing because it does not have a large alumni or another natural constituency that could become donors to the organization. Major national disease-related groups often rely heavily on acquisition mailings, based on the premise that they have a universal appeal. Almost everyone has a friend or family member who has had cancer, heart disease, or diabetes. When these groups reach out to the general public for donations, they will be fairly successful because the reader can identify with the cause.

So how does an organization determine whether acquisition mailing is right for it? Here are some questions to ask:

- Is there a compelling need to acquire new donors?
- Can the organization easily obtain names of individuals who would be potential supporters of our organization?
- Can the organization afford acquisition mailing?

The Need to Acquire New Donors

If the organization does not have a database of names and addresses, an acquisition mailing may be the way to go. It will identify individuals who have an interest in the organization. It will also provide unrestricted money in most cases. Often organizations that are dependent solely on grant fundraising find themselves in the position of being able to get specific programs funded through grants but not operating expenses. Direct mail can help solve this problem because typically direct mail donors are low-end donors who are not expecting that their gift will be directed to a specific program.

Acquiring Names for Direct Mail

There are several ways to acquire names for direct mail, including:

- Building the organization's own list.
- List sharing.
- List rental.

Building the organization's own list

Building the organization's own list is one strategy to consider. Often an organization will ask its board members, staff, or volunteers for names of their friends, relatives, or others they think may be interested in supporting this organization. This option may have its limitations because often board members and others do not want to "bug their friends" for money, so they may be reluctant to pass along names. If they do provide names, these friends and relatives may have little interest in the organization's mission.

On the other hand, relatives or friends of board members and volunteers often will contribute just because they are asked by someone they know.

Effective ways to build a mailing list include gathering names of individuals who:

- Attend the organization's special events.
- Visit the organization's Website.
- Attend programs sponsored by the organization.

This method is more effective than relying on staff and board members to provide lists because there is some level of certainty that these individuals have an interest in the programs of the organization.

List sharing

Some organizations are willing to share lists with other organizations that have a similar mission but may not be a direct competitor.

Of course, if the organization has no list to share in return, it may be hard to convince even a friendly organization to provide its list. Also, the *Donor Bill of Rights* and some state laws require that the organization planning to share its list must give donors the opportunity to opt out of having their name given to other organizations.

List rental

Renting lists of addresses may be effective for some groups. A list broker can provide names and addresses of individuals who may be interested in the organization. When deciding on potential list brokers, ask for several names of similar groups that have used this company previously. Call them. Ask specific questions about their experience with the company. Never deal with a company that does not provide references.

Make certain to obtain in writing the restrictions on the use of the names and addresses before you agree on a fee. List brokers will rent names usually for a one-time use or a time-limited use—say, one year—meaning that the organization can mail to these individuals as many times as they want within that specified time period.

The advantage of renting a list from a reputable list broker is that the organization can identify individuals with an interest in its cause. For example, an environmental group can rent lists of subscribers to outdoor magazines whose readers will likely be interested in protecting the environment. In addition, the names to be rented can be qualified in a number of ways, including household income, age, ethnicity, zip code, or owners of property. Be aware, however, that the more qualifiers put on the list the more expensive the rental charges will be.

Deciding on Acquisition Mailings

When considering acquisition mailing, be aware that the receipts often do not exceed expenditures. However, the long-term benefit of acquisition mailing often outweighs this initial cost because once an individual makes a gift, the donor becomes the organization's donor. Direct mail offers a tremendous opportunity to build a strong relationship with the donor that can result in renewed and increased gifts. Many major donors and even planned givers have started out by being approached through an acquisition mailing.

The most important thing to remember is that the organization must have a strategy to renew and upgrade donors acquired through this method. Be aware that the average response rate on acquisition mailings is 1/2 to 1 1/2 percent. On the other hand, sending direct mail to individuals who already know and support the organization usually yields a response of 10 to 20 percent.

The Direct Mail Package

Direct mail consists of more than just writing a letter. The whole package needs to be considered. The following also need to be determined:

- What will the outside (or carrier) envelope look like?
- Who will write the letter, who will sign the letter, and how lengthy should it be?
- What type of response form will be used?
- What other information should be included?
- Are the mailing lists accurate?

The outside envelope

The outside envelope is important because, if the package is not inviting, chances are the letter will not even be opened. Studies have shown that stamps typically get a better response than metered mail because the letter looks more personal. For small mailings, first-class stamps can be very effective. For large mailings and acquisition mail, nonprofit bulk rate stamps are often just as effective. A message or a photo on the outside envelope can encourage individuals to open mail.

When considering any type of direct mail, meet with the bulk mail staff of your post office. Consider advantages and disadvantages of bulk mail, first-class mail, and other choices. Also, meet with representatives of "mail houses." Often, your organization can save time and money by working with an established company, typically called a mail house, which mails to a large number of individuals. Often, a group such as a Retired Seniors Volunteer Program (RSVP) will stuff, stamp, and mail envelopes at a reasonable fee or sometimes as a volunteer service.

Because there is amazing technology available today, it is advisable not to use labels on the outside envelope. A personalized printing that looks like a hand-typed envelope or even a handwritten envelope is much more effective. Some organizations have been very successful in asking key community leaders to be the letter signers, to send the letter on their letterhead, and to use their personal envelopes.

The letter

Staff members should not sign the appeal letter. It is much more effective to have a high-profile community leader, preferably a board member or other volunteer with the organization, sign the letter. This immediately gives credibility to the organization and lets the reader know that the community supports this organization. As with the outside envelope, if the organization can secure the signer's personal letterhead it can be even more effective, especially with organizations that are not well known in their community. Make sure the letter is professionally written and tells the story of the organization. The volunteer can add personal touches to the letter before signing it.

In most states, fundraising mail appeals are also required to carry a statement that the organization is registered within the state to conduct fundraising. Be sure to check the requirements not only in the state in which the organization is located but in the states to which letters might be mailed.

The length of the letter varies depending on the audience. Many direct mail experts say a three- or four-page letter is the most effective. Some individuals, however, will not read more than a one-page letter. The organization should test a few approaches to see what its prospective donors respond to best. A good rule of thumb to follow is that the letter should be as long as it takes to tell the story. The story is drawn from the organization's case for support.

Always use a personalized inside address to the prospective donor. The first paragraph should be a "grabber" that will keep them interested in reading more. The letter must contain a call to action, or the "ask." It is always best to ask for a specific amount of money, to ask higher rather than lower, and to tell donors how their money will be used. A P.S. is often used to reiterate important concepts or to stress the urgency of the appeal.

Enclosures

Many organizations enclose brochures, photos, or token give-aways such as labels or bookmarks with the direct mail piece. Again, knowing the audience is critical to a successful mail appeal. Some individuals like the giveaways. Others have so many that they get annoyed when they receive these items or would rather see their money spent on the programs of the organization. It is important to test the audience and see which approach gets the best response.

The response piece

The response piece is the most important part of a direct mail package. The outside envelope, although important, is usually the first thing to get thrown away, followed by the letter, and then the enclosures. The one piece that individuals generally save the longest is the response envelope. It makes sense, therefore, to spend a lot of thought to what the response envelope and pledge card should look like. A larger response envelope (#9, 9 inches) stands out more than a smaller one (#6, 6 inches) and gives the opportunity for individuals to enclose larger checks (in inches, and sometimes in dollars). Various options should be provided for individuals to check off the amount of their gifts, starting with the highest amounts first.

Giving clubs, which are various levels of giving each with a name conveying the size of the gift, can be effective in encouraging individuals to consider moving up to a higher gift. These can also be listed with the amounts. Examples of giving clubs might include generic names such as the Founder's Circle, the President's Club, or the Century Club, or could be specific to the organization such as the Blue and Gold Club (school colors), or the Harris Society (founder of the organization). These names should be carefully thought out. Avoid naming giving clubs in a museum after specific artists, as some individuals may think the Picasso Circle is not as prestigious as the Degas Circle even though the contribution size is larger.

The mailing list

No matter how the organization obtains its mailing list, accuracy is of primary importance. Nothing turns off a potential donor more than being addressed improperly. A misspelled name, a Mr. and Mrs. salutation to individuals no longer married, or a Mrs. if the woman prefers to be addressed as Ms., can make the difference between a gift and having the letter tossed in the trash without even being opened. If the mailing list is internal, be sure it is kept up to date and reviewed before each mailing. If the list is being obtained from an outside source such as a list broker, ask the source how accurate it is, and ask this question to representatives of other organizations that have previously hired the company.

Renewal Mailings

Direct mail can be used to renew and upgrade donors. The organization should have a plan for how it will deal with first-time donors in order to build a relationship that leads to renewed and increased gifts. Some options might be:

- A special welcome packet sent to first-time donors, acknowledging that this is their first gift, providing them with additional information about the organization, and outlining the organization's need for continued support.

- A phone call to new donors from a staff or board member or a program participant thanking them for their gift.
- A thank-you letter sent within 24 hours of the gift being received.

Renewal mailings should always include the amount of the donor's last gift and a specific request for an increased gift. Be certain to let donors know that their previous gifts were appreciated and how the money was used to further the mission of the organization. The giving club concept can be very effective by asking the donor who, for example, has given $50 a year for the past three years to consider stepping up to the "Century Club" with a $100 gift. Small donors who are considered likely prospects for a larger gift should be called or visited.

Renewal and upgraded gifts through direct mail should be analyzed on an annual basis. Here are some questions to ask:

- How many donors renewed?
- How many donors upgraded?
- How many donors lapsed (did not renew)?
- What was the dollar increase in gifts?
- What were the costs of renewal mailings?
- What was the average gift size, and did it increase or decrease from previous mailings?
- Are individuals who gave more than a specific amount in the mail called or visited the next year?

How often should direct mail be sent to the same donor? This should be tested with donors. Do they respond better to more frequent or less frequent mailings? The organization's budget may dictate how frequently it will use direct mail. For many small organizations, once a year is sufficient for a direct mail appeal. Many organizations find that direct mail is effective at year-end (November or early December) when individuals are considering tax consequences of their charitable giving and are often in a more generous mood. Renewal mailings can also be used to encourage monthly giving with an option to contribute using a credit card or through PayPal.

Cultivation Mailings

Mail can be used in other ways to approach donors. Cultivation mailings such as program updates, newsletters, annual reports, and surveys can also be used to build relationships with donors. Individuals who care about an organization want to hear from their favorite nonprofit organization not just when they are asking for money. They want to know what the organization is doing, how it is helping the community, and perhaps even how they can become involved as a volunteer.

Newsletters

One good way to communicate with donors and potential donors is through a monthly or quarterly newsletter. The newsletter can be in hard copy, electronic, or both. Be sure that the newsletter actually contains "news," not the monthly lunch menu in the cafeteria. News can be:

- Program updates.
- Staff and board appointments.
- Personal stories from program participants.
- Personal stories from donors.
- Information about expanded programs and facilities.

All these are newsworthy items that can inspire and motivate donors. Most donors love to see their name in print, so list donors to the organization unless they have requested anonymity.

Photos should be used, but make sure they are good quality. In general, photos should be of no more than three or four people. Large group shots do not look professional in a newsletter. Leave white space. Do not try to fill every inch of the paper, and use fonts that are easy to read. Talk to a printer or an individual who is familiar with type styles to select the one that is appropriate for the material.

The newsletter should always prominently feature the organization's mission and vision statements, and board of directors list. A response envelope should be included for those who want to make a donation.

Annual Reports

The nonprofit organization's annual report does not have to look like the type of expensive publication General Motors or IBM sends its stockholders. An interesting and well-written annual report can be a great donor-cultivation tool. Most nonprofits are required to submit information annually to the Internal Revenue Service, and this information will be available to donors by searching the Internet. Why not use this opportunity for another communication and send it to donors and prospective donors? It is important that financial information included in the annual report is understandable by the readers.

Add some photos, stories about program successes, and the organization's plans for the future. Include the list of donors for the year. Send the annual report to all donors along with a note from the board chair telling donors that the organization wants to keep them apprised of the organization's status and plans.

Donor Surveys

Surveys can be an effective donor communication tool to find out what motivates donors to give, which programs they are interested in, and whether they might consider volunteering for the organization. Online surveys are the cheapest and easiest to use, and they tabulate the answers for you. Surveys can also be mailed. Most donors feel appreciated if the organization asks for their input.

Keep surveys short, simple, and easy to use. And of course, be sure that the information is easy to analyze and report and that it will actually be used to make changes within the organization where a change is indicated.

Acknowledgment Mailings

Donors should always be thanked within 24 hours of the time their donation is received. This goes a long way to providing donors with acknowledgment that their check was indeed received, but also letting the donor know that the organization values their relationship. A year-end tax receipt is always helpful, because many individuals may not save their original thank-you letter. Handwritten notes on the letters are a good way to show the donor that the organization really cares about them and knows them personally.

An occasional letter just to let the donor know how the organization is doing and how it is using the donor's contributions to truly make a difference is most welcome. It will help the organization build those lasting relationships that are so critical to successful fundraising.

Effective use of the mail can play a major role in helping to build a successful fundraising campaign.

Chapter 10
Telephone

Many organizations dread the "T" word, thinking telephone fundraising is something both callers and those being called hate. However, studies have proven that telephone fundraising is always more effective than direct mail campaigns. The secret is in how the telephone is used to create the relationships that will lead to major gifts. Statistics also show that most individuals do not complain to authorities about calls from individuals in their community raising funds for local nonprofits. They *do* complain about the storm window salespeople, credit card telemarketers, "robo-calls," and other similar calls. Nonprofits are exempt from the "Do Not Call" lists. However, in many states nonprofits are required to register to do telephone fundraising as well as other types of fundraising. If a professional firm is used, they are also required to register in most states that require nonprofit registration.

When Is It Appropriate to Initiate a Telephone Campaign?

Phone solicitation should always be used in the three-pronged approach recommended in this book. According to this approach, potentially major donors should be visited, mid-sized donors should be called, and those likely to give small amounts should be solicited by mail and the Internet. The organization may, in fact, establish criteria such that the top 10 percent of its donors are solicited in person, the next 40 percent receive a phone call, and the rest are contacted by mail or e-mail. Of course, a major factor in deciding in which pile to place prospective donors is the number of volunteers available to conduct visits, make calls, or stuff envelopes.

In addition to using the phone to solicit gifts, it may also be used for a number of other purposes, such as:

- To invite previous donors to upgrade their gifts.
- To ask for pledges to a capital campaign.
- To identify prospects for planned gifts.
- To survey donors about the case for support.
- To thank donors for their gifts.

Whom Do We Call?

The reason many organizations do not favor using the phone in their fundraising program is they think of telephone fundraisers as being the typical "telemarketers" who call during dinner, read a prepared script, and will not take no for an answer. The first rule of using the phone effectively for nonprofit fundraising is that the individuals receiving the call must know the organization. They are members, donors, or users of the organization's services. Never make cold calls to individuals who do not know the organization or have any affiliation with its mission.

How many prospects should be in the database to start a phone campaign? Phone appeals can be made to a few dozen, several hundred, or tens of thousands of individuals.

How are the calls made? One main factor is the number of individuals to be called. If, for example, the nonprofit is planning to call a group of a few dozen major donors to thank them for their gifts, the calls may be made by board members from their homes.

If several hundred members will be called to make pledges or renew or upgrade their membership, the organization might enlist a team of a few dozen volunteers to staff a phonathon. For a phonathon, all the callers are in the same room. They can use a "phone bank" or use their cell phones and make the calls. Many volunteers state that it is much easier to make a large number of calls when they are in a room with other friends who are also making calls. It is not a good idea to just give volunteers a long list of names to call from home when they have time. The organization will lose control of the process, and most volunteers, although they have good intentions, will never get around to making all of their calls.

However, if the organization has thousands of names to be called, it may be wise to engage a professional telephone fundraising firm to handle that volume. Or, when calling for a specialized purpose such as capital campaign or planned giving, a professional firm may be the answer.

Using Volunteers to Make Telephone Calls

Volunteers can include:

- Current users of the organization's services.
- Previous users of services.
- Current members or donors.
- Students.
- Alumni.
- Board members.
- Volunteers from local businesses or service clubs.

Each of these groups has something to offer to the organization. Students or individuals who benefit from the services provided by the organization can be excellent volunteers because they can effectively thank donors for their support and ask for continued support. Who can resist the call from a student who has received a scholarship from the organization, someone who has been a patient of the free clinic, or an individual who attends the art classes at the local community center?

Alumni, likewise, have a great deal of affection for their benefactors and can relate well to other alumni. Do not think of alumni only as graduates of a school. Most organizations have groups of individuals they can call alumni. One dog rescue group used this method effectively during a capital campaign when volunteers who had adopted dogs called their fellow "alumni" (other individuals who adopted a dog in the same year). The recipients of the calls immediately had a great rapport with the callers and responded well.

Board members and users of services know the programs well and can be very effective at translating the case into an "ask." Similarly, current members of the organization, perhaps attendees at the local orchestra's concerts, can also relate well to other concert goers.

Do not forget to encourage the participation of local businesspeople, such as bankers, real estate agents, insurance salespeople, and stockbrokers. Often these individuals do extensive phone calling in their business so they are not afraid to pick up the phone and "dial for dollars." Local service and professional clubs will often take on a project such as this to benefit a local charity as part of their community service work.

Calls should be made by volunteers rather than paid staff members. An exception to the rule might be when a staff member has a close personal relationship with a particular prospective donor.

Preparing for a Phonathon

Volunteers may not always be comfortable or skilled at asking for phone pledges. It is imperative that the volunteers be trained before putting them on the phone bank. First, they should be totally familiar with the organization and its programs, especially the particular project or program for which they are seeking funding. Often volunteers will be treated to a light meal while they view a video or PowerPoint presentation about the organization and its case.

A script or list of talking points will be critical. It is best not to have volunteers read directly from a canned script but rather to take the talking points and put them into their own words. They will sound more sincere and less like a telemarketer. They may want to use the script for the first few calls until they get into a rhythm, and to practice by calling a few good friends or relatives first.

Some tips on handling customary objections will also help them feel more at ease on the phone. Of course, be sure to instruct them not to use any high-pressure techniques to obtain pledges. They also need to be instructed on how to complete the phonathon forms and tally their totals.

A few incentives can make the volunteers feel appreciated. A low-cost item such as a T-shirt or coffee mug given to each caller at the end of the night is a good idea. And, of course, volunteers are often motivated by the competition of getting the most pledges, the largest pledge of the evening, or completing the most calls. Some nice items such as gift certificates to popular local restaurants can inspire volunteers to persist in their calling and not get discouraged.

Phonathon planning should always include a light meal for the volunteers. Do not make it a huge buffet, or they will spend the whole night eating and socializing instead of making calls. Serving pizza, sandwiches, or salads during the orientation period so they can eat while being trained is recommended. Be sure to have lots of water and other beverages available during the evening.

Using Professional Callers

In larger organizations, because of the large volume of names to be called or the amount of the "ask," it may make sense to hire a professional telephone fundraising firm to do the calling. Look for a professional telephone fundraising firm that has worked with nonprofits and will work on a flat-fee basis. The fee may be based on the number of calls completed or an hourly fee. According to the Association of Fundraising Professionals, percentage-based fundraising of any kind is unethical. Always stay away from these firms, which use high-pressure tactics and unethical practices.

Always interview several firms in person. Do not hire firms that are not willing to be interviewed or provide the names of previous clients. Ask at least three clients for the total amount raised. How much of that amount was kept by the nonprofit and how much was given to the fundraising firm? Were the clients happy with the professionalism of the firm? If there is a regulatory authority in the state, make sure the firm is registered before engaging it to do the phone campaign. Most professional firms will offer a variety of services such as sending the pre-call letter, making the follow-up contacts, preparing management reports showing the results of calls, and often writing copy for the letters and pledge forms. Most reputable firms will allow you to listen in on the calls they are making on behalf of the organization and change the script. They may even allow the organization to make selected calls.

If the organization does not have enough volunteers to make phone calls, another option to consider is sending out mail requests to individuals. Compare the potential receipts and expenditures between conducting a mail campaign and hiring a professional telephone fundraising firm.

The List

As with a direct mail appeal, having an accurate list is a critical part of the organization's success. Be sure you have correct names and phone numbers. Many individuals tend to be mobile. They get married and divorced, change their phone number, and even eliminate a landline and use a cell phone exclusively. If you feel the list is not accurate, spend some time cleaning it up. Services can be contracted to make sure addresses and phone numbers are accurate.

This can save a lot of time, money, and frustration on the part of volunteers, and also save money when using a professional telephone calling firm.

A pre-call mailing should always be used. This gives legitimacy to the call and can lay the groundwork for a successful call. Finding the right letter-signer is an important part of the process. Letters should be signed by a volunteer, preferably one with a high community profile that will be warmly received by the individual receiving the letter. If possible, the volunteer making the call should sign the letter.

Do not give individuals the option in the letter to send a donation "so they won't be called." It gives the donor the idea that the phone call is punishment for not sending in a donation. The letter should state that this is an important project so you want to talk to the donor personally about it. The letter and any supporting material should be based on the case for support.

The Calls

Volunteers should begin every call by saying that they are a volunteer for the organization. They should state whether they are involved as a board member, a past or present user of the service, or in another volunteer capacity. They should next remind the individual of the previously sent letter and ask if they have any questions. The caller should then ask the prospective donor about present involvement either with the agency or with agencies with similar missions. If it is an arts organization, ask about interest in the arts. If it is an organization serving children, the caller should ask if the prospective donor is aware of the need for these programs. The caller should next tell the prospect how much his or her interest and support of the organization are appreciated.

Both professional callers and volunteers should always ask for a specific pledge based on the donor's previous history with the organization and the caller's sense of the phone call. A phone appeal can be a very effective way to encourage a donor to upgrade to a higher level. For an initial gift, ask for the largest amount the donor is expected to give. For example, if you believe donors will give from $10 to $50, ask if they can pledge $50. For previous givers, start by asking for twice the amount of their previous gift. With larger donations, do not increase the ask amount too much; a 10-percent or 20-percent increase is usually appropriate. If using a professional firm, it will guide you through the process of setting ask amounts. If using volunteers, a fundraising consultant might help with the letter, the process of setting the amount to request, and the volunteer training.

Follow-Up

Even though volunteers are well trained, the prospective donor may have questions that the caller cannot answer. If this is the case, be sure a process is in place to get back to the donor either by phone or mail with the information requested. Some donors may prefer not to be called. If they request to be removed from future phonathon lists, be sure to honor this request and make note of their preference on the database so they are not called in the future. Be sure that the callers thank donors for their past support. Callers should always graciously thank the individuals they have called for their time, whether or not they have made a pledge. It is important to lay the groundwork for a future "ask." Remember: a no is not always "no forever."

Collecting pledges after a phonathon is obviously an important step. One practice that helps collection rates tremendously is sending out the pledge forms the very next day. Include a return envelope so individuals can easily write a check and drop it in the mail. All the forms should be prepared the night of the phonathon. If a professional firm is being used, it will handle this. For a volunteer phonathon, usually some volunteers do not like to make phone calls. They can be asked to help with tallying results and preparing the pledge confirmations for mailing.

Integrating Phone Calls Into the Overall Fundraising Plan

Phone appeals are important because they allow the organization to build relationships with the donors—relationships that will help move them up the donor pyramid. Using information from the phone program in the overall development program is critical. First, be sure to record any address or name changes, those who wish to be removed from future phone lists, donors who want to remain anonymous, or any other pertinent information gained during the call. A good caller will often elicit valuable insights that can help in future solicitations with donors, such as their interest in a particular program. All of this information needs to be entered into the donor database along with the amount of the pledge.

Remember: Do not always use the phone just to ask for money. A thank-a-thon, in which donors are called simply to thank them for their donations, is an extremely useful tool in building those lasting relationships. Try it. The organization will gain friends and future major donors!

Chapter 11
Special Events

Walks, runs, galas, golf tournaments, rubber ducky races. What are these events all about, how does a nonprofit run one, and which one is right for the organization? How many events should be run each year?

There are several reasons special events are popular fundraisers for nonprofits, among them:

- Almost any organization can run a special event.
- The money raised from events can go into unrestricted operating costs of the organization, because most event attendees do not expect that their event money will fund a particular program.
- Events are an excellent way to raise awareness of the organization.

On the other hand, there are some important negative concerns to be considered:

- They are very labor-intensive for the staff.
- They require a large number of volunteers.
- Being invited to attend too many events can cause "donor fatigue."
- Volunteers can get burned out by attending and working at events.
- Special events can actually lose money if not run properly.

Some typical events run by nonprofits include:

- "Thons."
  - ➢ Walkathons.
  - ➢ Marathons.
  - ➢ Dance-a-thons.
  - ➢ Bike-a-thons.
  - ➢ Bowl-a-thons.
- Dinners.
  - ➢ Galas.
  - ➢ Award dinners.
  - ➢ Testimonial dinners.
  - ➢ Roasts.
- Sports events.
  - ➢ Golf tournaments.
  - ➢ Tennis tournaments.
  - ➢ Bowling tournaments.
- Auctions.
  - ➢ Silent auctions.
  - ➢ Online auctions.
  - ➢ Live auctions.
- Other events.
  - ➢ Festivals/fairs.

➤ Open-house events.

➤ House parties.

➤ Health fairs.

➤ Wine-tasting events.

➤ Rodeos.

➤ Concerts.

➤ Office Olympics.

➤ Horse, pig, balloon, hospital bed, and auto races.

➤ Recognition events for volunteers, donors, and staff.

- And many more!

Tips for Successful Special Events

One important factor that makes a big difference in the success or failure of an event is its planning. A nonprofit organization needs to think carefully about some of the following factors that go into event planning:

- Are volunteers enthusiastic about the event?
- Will the board support the event?
- Does the staff have time to manage all the details?
- How many other organizations in the community are holding similar events?
- Is this event something constituents will support?
- How much "seed money" is needed to fund the startup?
- How much can the organization reasonably expect to net?
- What are the total costs to run the event, including staff time?
- Is there sufficient time to plan?
- Does this event fit the mission of the organization?

During the planning process, it is often helpful to check with other organizations that have conducted similar events to see what successes and problems they have had. They may even be willing to share some of their materials that can then be adapted for a new event.

Volunteer Committees

Fundraising events should always involve a volunteer committee to help plan and implement it. The size of the committee will vary depending on the event. Events may involve a committee of 10 or 100 or more volunteers. A golf tournament, for example, generally has a chair and a few committee members who will secure prizes, a publicity chair, a facilities chair who will work on the arrangements for the golf course, a refreshment chair, a subcommittee to recruit foursomes to play in the tournament, and a sponsorship subcommittee. A weeklong block party may have hundreds of volunteers working at booths in two- or three-hour shifts.

No matter what type of event, there are a few things to consider:

- Make sure volunteers are aware of the goals of the event. (Is this a fundraising event or a friend-raising event?) If it is a fundraising event, what are the dollar goals? If a friend-raiser, what is the goal for the number of individuals attending, and what information does the organization want the participants to receive?

- Every volunteer must have a job description outlining the expectations and the time frame involved.

- The organization must provide the volunteers with the tools they need to do their job. They may need special training, staff support such as handling the event registrations, or special technology to make their job easier.

- Volunteers should be carefully matched to the skill set required for this event. For example, if the event requires a master of ceremonies, does the organization have a volunteer who is experienced and comfortable with public speaking?

Before embarking on an event, it will be necessary to know how many volunteers will be needed, what type of volunteers will be needed, and whether the organization can reasonably expect to recruit a sufficient number of volunteers with the skills needed to implement this event.

Board Support

Another critical factor in deciding which events to run is the level of support that can be expected from the board. For example, if planning a black-tie gala dinner dance in a posh hotel, can board members afford to attend, and will they sell tickets to their friends? Events such as award dinners or dinners with a silent auction can be very effective, but individuals will notice if board members are not in attendance. Board members should be willing to host a table, get a foursome to play golf, or sponsor a bowling team. If they are not "on board" with the event, the organization needs to find an event that is more likely to be supported by the board.

Staff Time

No matter how dedicated and enthusiastic the volunteers and board are about the event, staff always must be both willing and able to devote a great deal of time to managing the event (and the volunteers). Staff will be needed to assist volunteers in handling registration for the event, mailing out invitations, and sorting and storing prizes. One consideration is how much time this event will take away from other tasks that staff could or should be doing. Be sure to have adequate staff before launching a special event.

Competition

Many communities have dinner dances and golf tournaments every week, and the community can get burned out by too many of the same type of events. Even if the organization comes up with a novel idea for an event, after a few years, especially if it is extremely successful, other agencies will steal the idea and run similar events. Before planning an event, investigate who else in the community is running similar events, for how many years, and what their track record is for a successful event.

Timing is critical. Are there other competing events on the same day? Sometimes the agency can join forces with other organizations to have one large event (more about this in Chapter 17 under "Collaborative Events").

Community Support

One of the main considerations is whether the community will support this event. If individuals feel there are too many galas, golf tournaments, and runs already, they may not support one more. Some companies have established guidelines that prohibit sponsorship of all events or certain types of events, or they are simply bombarded with too many requests and eliminate all sponsorships. Ask some of the organization's donors and board members if their employers would sponsor this event. Some individuals may limit the number of events they will attend annually. Because all special events cost money, individuals may not attend events they feel are too expensive. A survey of constituents can be helpful when deciding whether to conduct an event.

Planning Time

It is also critical to make sure to allow enough time to plan the event. Most events take about a year to plan. Some facilities, special entertainment, or guest speakers may need to be booked far in advance. Usually the planning for next year's event starts with the debriefing after the current year's activity. It is wise to have a co-chair of the event who will take over the chair position the following year so that event planning will be seamless.

Mission-Related Events

The most successful events are those that are closely related to the mission of the organization. For example, the local 4H Club could be very successful with a "Kiss a Pig" contest or cow chip bingo. However, the local art museum's patrons would not be likely to relate to this type of event, and would probably rather attend a gala dinner in the art galleries of the museum.

Before deciding on an event, think about how well it relates to the mission. Will it help attract the individuals who are likely to be donors of the organization? Will it inform individuals of the value of the organization's mission?

Some Pitfalls to Avoid

Consider the following before deciding on what type of event to run:

- Is this event likely to be adversely affected by bad weather (an outdoor concert for instance)?

- Is it possible to insure against losses at the event (for example, hole-in-one insurance for a golf tournament)?

- Are there risks inherent with celebrity involvement (hidden expenses in the contract, and so forth)?

- Will this event have any fallout with donors (a politically incorrect comedian, for example)?

- Does the event require any seed money the organization cannot afford?

- Is there a chance this event could lose money, and if so, can the organization afford that loss?

Choosing the Right Event for the Organization

So, how does an organization find the right event? The following questions will help the decision-making process:

- Does this event fit with and promote the mission?
- How much can be raised?
- How much does the organization need to spend?
- Are there volunteers available who know anything about running this type of event?

- Will the board members attend, sell tickets, and sponsor the event?
- How much staff time is involved, and is there a staff person with the skills to manage the event?
- Will this type of event help raise community awareness of the organization?
- Will donors and friends support this event?
- What risks does this event have and is the organization prepared to handle them?

A Word About Collaborative and Third-Party Events

If the organization does not feel it has the capability to run a major event, several other options should be considered. Collaboration with another organization should be researched, especially with organizations that have a similar but not directly competing mission. One word of caution when embarking on collaborative events is to make sure that both organizations are willing to sign an agreement outlining how expenses and income will be shared, and how the workload will be divided.

Another option is a third-party event, in which another group holds an event and gives the proceeds to the organization. Again, a written agreement should be in place outlining exactly how income and expenses are to be shared. The event organizers should clearly tell the recipient organization how its name, logo, and other information will be used to promote this event.

With the proper written agreement, both third-party events and collaborative events can be very successful for organizations that do not have the staff, time, volunteers, or expertise to run an event on their own.

Avoiding Special Event Overload

Perhaps the organization is already conducting multiple events and needs to decide which ones to continue and which ones to drop. Using the list of questions on page 127 and 128 should help decide which events are the most appropriate for the organization.

If the staff is bombarded with requests from board members and volunteers to add yet another special event to its bag of fundraising tricks, take heed! Many organizations get caught up in "special event fever" when a board member or another well-meaning volunteer hears about a successful event run by another organization and decides that this organization should run a similar event. The first thing to do is help the board understand that each proposed event must be closely examined to be sure that the benefits outweigh the costs—*including lost opportunity costs*. Unless staff members are hired exclusively to run special events, staff members who are supposed to be providing programs and services may be diverting their energies by running events. Board members and volunteers need to understand that, if staff members are busy with events, it may keep them from visiting major donors, meeting grant deadlines, and raising money in other ways.

Special events are just one way of raising money for the organization and may not be the most productive or cost-effective way. Board members often opt for events because it relieves them of the burden of directly asking others to support the organization. When it comes to the various types of fundraising and the average costs of each method, special events often rank low on the ladder of effectiveness.

It is usually recommended that nonprofits hold one signature event each year. Events should, whenever possible, tie in to the mission of the organization. For example, a homeless shelter may invite local businesspeople to share breakfast with the shelter guests before the business community is asked to support the shelter financially. The goals of the event must be clear to all involved. Is it a friend-raiser, a fundraiser, or both? There should always be a careful analysis done *before* undertaking an event to set specific objectives and *after* the event to see if the objectives have been met.

Planning and accurate recordkeeping are essential. Track not only how many individuals bought tickets, but who volunteered for which tasks and how reliable they were. After each event, an evaluation meeting should be held involving all of the committee members to review what went right and what went wrong when it is fresh in everyone's mind. Make sure to ask some participants to rank the event, not only the organizers. Keep information in written form to pass on to next year's event committee.

Perhaps the best way to avoid overdependence on special events is to have a well-thought-out development plan that encompasses all types of fundraising activities. The board of directors should have input into the development of this plan. If they have bought into the plan, they are less likely to want to deviate from it. Having a solid plan has enabled many organizations to avoid the temptation to add one more event to their list, and encourages a focus on more productive ways to raise money.

Chapter 12
Fundraising Dinners

Many organizations find that a dinner is an effective fundraising event. One type of fundraising dinner is a testimonial dinner, honoring an individual while raising funds for the organization. Begin the planning by selecting an individual or individuals worthy of being honored.

Examples might include:

- An individual who has been particularly important in the founding or history of the organization.
- A group of program participants being honored (for example, students graduating from an educational program).
- An individual who is reaching a particular milestone (25 years as executive director, for example).
- A winner of a particular award (such as volunteer of the year).

- An important individual in the organization who is celebrating a particular birthday or anniversary.

Select an honoree or honorees with these characteristics:

- They are beloved individuals, so that large numbers of friends would be likely to attend a dinner honoring them.
- They would be willing to provide large numbers of names and addresses of individuals to be invited.
- Many of their family members and friends have the financial ability to contribute to the organization.

As with any event, careful planning is critical to success. The following planning steps will be needed:

- **Get board buy-in.** Before deciding to go ahead, get a commitment from the board that all members will attend, encourage others to attend, and financially support the event. It is important that some board members assist in planning the event.
- **Get a commitment from the honoree.** The honoree must agree to provide an extensive list of individuals to invite and to make a short speech at the event.
- **Select a date and location.** The date should be set far enough in advance to permit sufficient planning. The date for many major events is set one to two years in advance.
- **Secure a location that is suitable for the audience you are anticipating.** A local community center may be an ideal venue for some audiences. Hotels generally will be more expensive and you will need to get firm costs on food and drink. However, the audience may prefer this type of setting.
- **Form the event planning committee:**
  - ➤ The committee chair should ideally be a board member who is a good friend of the honoree.
  - ➤ The committee chair should have experience in chairing this type of event.
  - ➤ The event planning committee should be as large as possible.

Include many different segments of the community on the event planning committee, including:

- Close friends of the honoree.
- Relatives of the honoree.
- Active board members.
- Community leaders.
- Businesspeople.
- Wealthy individuals.
- Members of the honoree's religious institution.
- Individuals who share the honoree's hobby (for example, golf partners or club members).
- Representatives of different groups in the community (ethnic, religious, ages, professions).

Budget Items to Be Considered

Sponsorships

Ask individuals, businesses, and organizations to serve as sponsors for the dinner. Include political and other community leaders as well as wealthy individuals. Sponsors will be asked to pay a higher price to attend the dinner than other attendees. They should be listed on the invitation in order to show the level of support for this event and encourage individuals to attend.

Cost of Dinner

Some planning committees set a high dinner price in order to raise funds for the organization. Others set a lower dinner price and then solicit funds at the dinner. Think this through carefully. You do not want to set the dinner cost too high, or you will discourage attendance. On the other hand, some individuals do not like being solicited at an event after they have already paid to attend. Knowing the audience preferences will help determine the best approach. Take a look at the experiences of past dinners, and ask some potential attendees what they would prefer.

Complimentary Tickets

Think carefully about giving complimentary dinner tickets to individuals you would like to attend, including:

- Staff members who have a relationship with the honoree.
- Selected family members of the honoree.
- Media representatives.
- Other individuals whom you would like to attend.

Food and Drink

Discuss items such as whether there should be a reception before the dinner; whether alcoholic beverages should be served (and, if so, whether there will be an open bar or a cash bar): whether the dinner should be served or buffet; the menu selection, including whether there will be more than one choice of entrée served; and arrangements for individuals with dietary restrictions.

Program Ads

Every individual invited to the dinner should be asked if they would like to place an ad or a listing in the program book. In addition, businesses in the community and organizations to which the honoree belongs should be asked to place an ad in the dinner program.

The request for ads should include the following:

- Size of ad.
- Cost of ad.
- Deadline.
- Specifications for graphics such as company logos.
- Any additional charge for setting copy.

One important goal of any fundraising dinner is to have all the event costs including the dinner paid for before the dinner begins. There are many ways to do this, including:

- Ask a local printer to print the invitation, the program announcement, the ad book, and the pledge cards at no charge. In return, they will not be charged for their ad in the ad book and their contribution will be noted in the program book.

- Find a professional photographer in the community who will take pictures at the event at no charge and give him or her a free ad in the ad book.

- See if free entertainment can be secured, perhaps a church choir or school orchestra.

- Ask a potential large donor, whether an individual, business, or foundation to pay for all costs (for example, food, postage, plaques, room rental fees).

- If the event is not held in a hotel, ask the local vocational technical school to prepare and serve the dinner at no charge as a school project.

The Invitation

Prepare a formal invitation to the event. Send the invitation at least six weeks before the event with a response form and return envelope to:

- The mailing list submitted by honoree.
- Community leaders.
- Board and staff members.
- Program volunteers.
- Program participants and their families.
- Past program participants and their families.
- Media representatives.
- Political officials.

The invitation should include a card to enable individuals not attending the dinner to make a contribution to the organization in the honoree's honor. If pledges will be requested at the dinner, state in the invitation that "Pledges of support for the [name of the organization] will be accepted at the dinner."

The Program

Consider the following for the event program:

- Reception, which might be only for the honoree, his or her invited guests, and major sponsors.
- Welcome by the board chair.
- Brief introduction of head table and honored guests, including the honoree's family.
- Invocation. (Non-denominational and inclusive language is critical in order not to offend anyone.)
- Dinner.
- Description of agency services.
- Brief talk by an individual who has benefited from the program.
- Showing of a short video of the program or a Microsoft PowerPoint slide show.
- Introduction of the honoree.
- Brief talk by the honoree that includes a description of why the agency's services are important.
- Presentation of gift to the honoree.
- Request for pledges (if the invitation stated that requests for funds will be made at the dinner). This may be led by a different individual than the board chair. Pledge cards should already be placed on the dinner table.
- Dessert.
- Entertainment.

After the Dinner

Send a letter to every individual who was invited to the dinner but did not attend. Include:

- A description of the event.
- A picture of the honoree at the dinner with an important community figure.
- The total amount raised by the event.
- A statement of the wonderful things that can be accomplished if additional funds can be raised.
- A pledge card.
- A return envelope.

Send a thank-you letter to those who made pledges. Request that a check to pay the pledge be sent promptly or indicate how the pledge can be paid by credit card. Make certain to state exactly how to make the check out and include the address of the organization. Remember to include a statement of the amount of the contribution that is tax-deductible.

Other Variations

The dinner as described in this chapter is just one of numerous fundraising techniques. Have a full discussion of the options when the event planning committee meets so they can select the best event for the organization. Other possibilities include:

- **Time of day:** Hold fundraising breakfasts, luncheons, or receptions rather than dinners.
- **Fundraising activities at the dinner:** Many organizations have silent or live auctions at the event.
- **Honoree roast:** Rather than the traditional event at which only positive things about the honoree are said, some groups "roast" the honoree by saying humorous things about the honoree. Select this option only if three characteristics are present:

> ➤ An honoree who will not be offended no matter what is said about him or her.

> ➤ An honoree who has personal characteristics that are amusing.

> ➤ An individual or group of "roasters" who have the skill of "roasting" the honoree in a tasteful manner.

Have fun, honor an individual who deserves being honored, publicize the benefits of the organization, and raise funds—all in the same evening!

Chapter 13
Open-House Events

Friend-raising events can also be important for an organization. An open house is just one example of a friend-raiser, at which the organization is trying to raise awareness, not money.

If the program is located in a building such as a daycare center, a job-training program, or any building with on-site programs, holding an open house is an excellent way to create community awareness of the organization or to publicize the organization at the beginning of a fundraising campaign.

Invitation List

Consider carefully whom you would like to invite. The local chamber of commerce can provide the name of the heads of all the major businesses in town. Collect lists of major donors to other local campaigns. The local symphony, college or university, hospital, and United Way may be able to provide a program book that lists the names of large (and often small) donors. Some of these lists may even be available on these organizations' Websites, and someone will need to look up addresses for these individuals. Board and staff members should also be asked to provide lists of individuals who they believe will have an interest in the program. Invite all past donors.

Developing a Planning Committee

A large planning committee should be selected when holding an open house. Often planning committee members will come up with excellent ideas for what should be included. Include representatives of businesses, local governments, philanthropists, and religious organizations on the planning committee.

Because every community is different, the committee can suggest the best time of day to hold an open house and what the menu might include. Many open houses are informal, and only hors d'oeuvres are served. Others are more formal and include a breakfast or lunch.

Members of the planning committee should be asked to underwrite the costs of the open house or suggest who might do so. A well-selected planning committee should be able to provide lists of wealthy individuals or representatives of philanthropic businesses who can be invited and contacted for future donations.

Sending the Invitation

A professionally printed invitation should be mailed to each invitee. Make sure all names are spelled correctly, and titles and addresses are correct. Follow-up e-mails or phone calls by members of the planning committee, board, or staff members are appropriate.

Before the Open House

When individuals respond that they will be attending the open house, send them an acknowledgment from the board chair saying that he or she looks forward to seeing them. Decide whether to include information about the organization. Be sure the facility is in top-notch condition and that staff are briefed about their role in the open house.

At the Open House

Try to have enough greeters at tables to welcome each attendee and make sure to confirm that their name, position, address, phone number, and e-mail address are correct. Give each attendee a pre-printed name tag with his or her name (and company or organization) in as large a type print as possible. The name badge should be on a neck lanyard or have a clip because many individuals will not use stick-on name tags.

Each visitor should be greeted warmly and immediately by a board or staff member. Make sure that pictures are taken of visiting dignitaries for use in future publicity.

Meet and Greet

A reception period of perhaps a half hour should be held before the program. The board chair should greet every individual personally. All board members should circulate so no guest is alone. The planning committee will determine what type of refreshments will be served. This will depend on the time of the day. Is it a breakfast, daytime, or after-hours event? The planning committee should try to get refreshments donated by a local restaurant or caterer. Often these businesses will be happy to donate in exchange for permission to put their business cards on the refreshment table.

Program

Guests will then be assembled for a brief program. The chairs can be set theater-style or at round tables. The program should be scripted to the minute and should not last longer than 30 minutes. No request for funds is included in the program. Requests for funds can come at a later date. The program should highlight the services and the clients of the organization.

The program should include the following:

- A short welcome by the board chair, who introduces board members, staff members, and dignitaries.
- A video or PowerPoint presentation of five minutes or less highlighting the program.
- A personal story by a program participant or a family member of a participant explaining how the program has assisted him or her.
- If the crowd is a manageable size, a brief discussion period during which attendees are asked for their ideas on how to better publicize the organization, how they might be interested in partnering, or other ideas they have for the organization.
- Thanks for attending from the board chair.

The personal story from an individual receiving the agency's services is the most important part of the program. The presenter should be carefully selected and should be coached to keep the presentation brief but compelling.

Meal

At an open house there may be no formal meal served, but tables should be provided for guests to enjoy their refreshments with ease. Here are a few tips to keep in mind:

- At least one board member should be assigned to sit at each table.

- Before the meal or refreshments are served, begin with an interfaith prayer led by a religious leader who is advised that the prayer should reflect the fact that there may be many religious beliefs represented in the audience.
- Tables may be set with cloth tablecloths and napkins, silverware, and glasses, or more casually for an informal atmosphere.
- At the table, board and staff members should talk about program successes.

Another option is serving light refreshments in more of a cocktail-party setting. A microphone and podium should be placed in the front of the room so it will be relatively easy to get the attention of guests when it is time to start the program.

Open-House Follow-Up

As soon as possible after the open house, send a note under the board chair's signature to all attendees, thanking them for attending. Also send a note to those who did not attend. Include a picture from the event and state that individuals may arrange for a private tour.

Be sure to include attendees on the mailing list for newsletters and future solicitations. Think of the contacts you made at this event and how you can involve them in the organization at a later date.

Chapter 14
Raising Funds Through the Internet

Raising money through electronic media is an essential element of fundraising. The wise nonprofit organization therefore will develop a strategy for Internet fundraising that is designed to grow along with their organization.

There are several tools to use the Internet effectively in fundraising:

- The organization's Website.
- E-mail fundraising.
- Social networking sites.

It is important to understand that it is not just young people who are using the Internet. The number of individuals of all ages using the Internet is growing. The uses of the Internet for fundraising are also growing. Internet fundraising is being used for capital campaigns, endowment campaigns, special project campaigns, and planned giving campaigns, as well as the annual fund. In general, larger nationally known organizations are more successful at online fundraising simply because they have awareness among larger numbers of individuals, but even small organizations can benefit from having an up-to-date Website that encourages online donations.

The Organization's Website

The organization's Website is probably the easiest place to start and has the most potential to raise money. Take a look at the current Website—or, better still, have an outside party review it and provide an honest assessment of its effectiveness.

It is amazing to see the low quality of many nonprofit Websites. Perhaps a well-meaning volunteer has offered to "do a Website" for the organization. The organization must ask itself: Does this individual have the background and experience in designing a Website to make it work effectively? It will be worth the cost to have the Website designed by an expert in nonprofit fundraising and updated professionally.

Here are some general rules for Website design:

- Make it appealing.
- Make it interactive.
- Provide useful information.
- Keep it up to date.
- Make it easy to donate.
- Do not forget the basic information about the organization.

Good photographs of individuals involved in the program or stock photos that represent the types of clients served will instantly tell the viewer what the organization does. Do not use large group photos that are hard to see. Use good close-up face shots or action shots showing the type of activities the organization provides. Tell some personal stories about the individuals being helped. Look at some Websites of similar organizations. Note their positive and negative qualities. Share these with the Web designer.

Interactive Websites get far more return visits than those that are static. Allow individuals to answer a quick poll about a subject that relates to the organization. For example, ask visitors to the site about a local or national issue that affects the clients. Invite individuals to take a survey or to sign up for events online. Provide them with information they can download—the Seven Warning Signs of Cancer for a health-related organization or Ten Things You Can Do to Stop Global Warming for an environmental group, for example.

Keeping the Website up to date is critical. If individuals visit a Website in October and see an event listed that was held in February of the previous year, they will likely not come back again. Someone must constantly monitor and update the events and activities that are time-related.

Using the Website to raise money can be a great way for organizations that do not have a lot of time or staff to do other types of fundraising. Individuals cannot be expected to donate unless it is a simple process. Statistics prove that individuals may only click two or three times. If they do not find what they are looking for, they will move on. Have a "Donate Now" button on the home page that allows the visitor to donate online easily, using a credit card or a service such as PayPal. Of course, Internet fundraising should be just one strategy in the overall fundraising plan.

Do not forget to put basic information on the Website. Many nonprofit organizations do not list their address, their phone number, and an e-mail address for individuals wanting to contact the organization. Think about the organization's brochure, and be sure to include information that would be on any piece of printed material. The address and phone number should be on the home page as well as a "Contact Us" button, which points to staff e-mail addresses and multiple locations, with maps if needed. A list of board members also adds credibility to anyone wanting to know more about the organization. The mission and vision statements and the annual report should be prominently featured.

E-mail Fundraising

E-mail fundraising is much less expensive than direct mail. The first e-mail gift received from a donor may be only $10, but subsequent gifts will generally be larger, just as with direct mail. Use mail and e-mail to direct individuals to the Website. Ask them to make a gift after visiting the site, reviewing the information presented, and clicking the "Donate Now" button.

Some critical considerations for online fundraising are:

- The appeal must demonstrate a compelling need.
- The Website must be attractive and functional.
- Information of value must be provided.
- The ability to accept donations online is required.
- The ability to collect e-mail addresses and use them should be considered.

A compelling need, information of value, and demonstrated outcomes should be part of the case for support. The Website, offline communications, and proactive e-mail are critical. Perhaps the most challenging part of the equation is the ability to collect and use e-mail addresses effectively. Some ways to gather e-mail addresses include:

- Asking visitors to the Website to register in order to obtain information.
- Publishing an e-newsletter and asking hard copy newsletter subscribers to provide their e-mail addresses in order to save the organization money and provide them with more timely information.
- Asking for e-mail addresses when individuals purchase event tickets.

E-mail fundraising will get better results if the organization can:

- Keep the e-mail short.
- Make it graphically appealing.
- Give individuals an opportunity to opt out of future e-mail solicitations.

- Send the e-mail with a personal address.
- Have the signer of the e-mail be an individual the recipient knows.

Internet fundraising is important, but in many cases it will take several years to develop an online fundraising program that pays off.

Social Networking Sites

Many individuals—not just young people—are using social networking sites to connect with other like-minded people. The statistics on the growth of networking are impressive. Many nonprofits are setting up additional Websites on the social networking sites in order to increase their exposure. Link these sites to the organization's Website.

Also, consider networking venues such as Linked In and Plaxo, which many donors may use to connect with each other, and tell their friends and associates about the organization.

The possibilities are endless. Be sure to talk to an individual who is savvy in this field to get the organization started in Internet fundraising. Use Internet fundraising as an essential part of your fundraising portfolio.

Chapter 15
Planned Giving

Planned giving generally refers to any gift in which the donor is making a decision to support an organization with a larger gift than he or she would normally give annually. Most often this is done in the form of a "deferred gift," or one that the organization will not realize immediately. In large organizations, many different instruments may be used in its planned giving program, including charitable remainder trusts, annuities, gifts of appreciated stock, gifts of real estate, life insurance, and many more. For most small organizations, planned giving will be almost exclusively received in the form of bequests. In fact, bequests usually account for about 90 percent of all the organizations' planned gifts.

How does the small organization take advantage of the large generational transfer of wealth that will account for many charitable bequests? A good way to start is by establishing a planned giving committee. Include an attorney or financial consultant with expertise in this area. Remember that not all attorneys are well versed in planned giving. A litigator will not have extensive knowledge of planned giving vehicles, so look for the experts who work in the field of estate planning. With the guidance of these individuals, review the large number of different instruments and select a few that will relate to the individuals in the community. Check with similar organizations in the community and see what success they have had.

Develop a brochure that explains the options in simple terms. Clearly outline the benefits and risks of each type of giving opportunity. Show the benefit to the agency's service recipients as well as to the donor. Several companies have materials available that can be customized for each organization.

The committee should develop a plan for review by staff and board members that publicizes the different opportunities. Once individuals express an interest, refer them directly to the attorney or accounting expert, who will develop a plan to meet their specific needs. As with any type of fundraising, a planned giving program should start by asking the board to make a planned gift.

Memorial Giving

One effective way of raising funds is to set up a program whereby donors can encourage giving memorial funds to the organization. It is common when hearing of the death of a friend or family member to make a contribution to a related nonprofit organization.

The process is standard. Ask the family of the deceased to list in the obituary notice that contributions can be made to the organization in memory of their loved one. When a contribution is received, two notes are sent out immediately: A note is sent to the donor acknowledging the gift. A note is also sent to the next-of-kin of the deceased noting the name and address of the donor but not the amount of the gift.

Once the program is established, the organization should notify board, staff, donors, members, and the community that it has such a program.

Memorial Plaque

Another fundraising opportunity is the establishment of a memorial plaque in a prominent location at the agency. For a set fee, the family of the deceased can have the name of the deceased and the date of death included on a permanent memorial. Religious institutions often use this method very effectively.

Death of a Community Leader

The planned giving committee should have a set of procedures that will be put in place upon the death of a dedicated board member, staff member, or a member of the community who has supported the organization. Immediately after hearing of the death, the committee chair should approach the next-of-kin and ask for permission to establish a memorial fund at the agency in memory of the deceased. The next-of-kin is asked to include in the obituary that the family requests that contributions be made to the memorial fund at the agency.

As soon as possible, the agency mails an announcement notifying everyone on the mailing list of the death of the individual. The next-of-kin may give addresses of the deceased's family members and friends, who will also be sent the announcement. The announcement requests individuals to make contributions to the memorial fund. Often, the funds are earmarked for a specific interest of the deceased (for example, a scholarship fund). Follow-up notices are included in the agency's newsletter and other publicity materials for at least a year after the death. Often, an agency will request donations to the memorial fund on each anniversary of the individual's death.

Bequest Program

A bequest program is the most successful planned giving program for many organizations. It is a program any organization can initiate. Many times, individuals who would like to give large sums to the organization find themselves unable to do so in their life-time because of financial reasons. However, they are willing to make a bequest because they realize that many of their assets (such as their home) will have appreciated in value. Often, individuals who have established a will in which bequests are made only to spouses or children will revise their wills when they are older to also include nonprofit organizations.

This program can be initiated by having an attorney agree to change existing wills at no cost for members and supporters of the organization who want to make a bequest to the organization. This is an easy sell to any attorney, because often the individual will ask the same attorney to counsel the individual regarding estate plan-ning and perform other legal services at the attorney's normal fee. In some instances, the individual will not have a will and the at-torney will write a will for the client. The attorney may also offer a seminar on the advantages of having wills.

Individuals who have wills are encouraged to change them to include a bequest to the organization. The attorney assists the do-nor to change that individual's will to include a specific dollar bequest or a percentage of the estate as a bequest to the organiza-tion. The organization is notified of the bequest but often not the specific amount. When the individual dies, the executor of the estate makes arrangements to send the funds to the organization in accordance with the instructions in the bequest.

The organization should publicize the bequest program in agency newsletters, on mail appeals, on the Website, and in other public-relations programs. As in other forms of fundraising, board and staff members should be the first ones to be invited to leave a bequest to the organization in their will.

Organizations with a well-thought-out planned giving pro-gram have found that it is an excellent way to raise funds in the long run.

Chapter 16
Capital Campaigns

What is a capital campaign and when is it needed? A capital campaign is an intense effort on the part of a nonprofit organization to raise significant dollars in a specified period of time. Usually the money raised is to fund the construction, purchase, or renovation of a building. In some cases, campaigns are initiated to fund extraordinary expenditures of a capital nature, such as an expensive piece of equipment for a hospital or a new fire truck for a fire company.

Sometimes the campaign's focus is on building a permanent fund for maintaining or expanding programs. This is done by the establishment of an endowment fund. The agency keeps the principal in the bank and draws on the interest to fund program expenses. It is important to remember that the focus of the campaign should not be on the building or amassing a large endowment fund but on the benefits to the community that this facility or endowment will provide through expanded, increased, or more efficient programming.

Most capital campaigns use an outside consultant because, for most organizations, this is the largest amount of money they have ever raised and they are usually dealing with a tight time line. Most organizations do not have the expertise to deal with a capital campaign on their own.

First the organization needs to decide whether a campaign is needed, how much money must be raised, and whether or not it is ready for a campaign. Any discussion of a capital campaign should start with the strategic planning process. The board and staff must evaluate the organization's needs for programs and services.

In the planning process, questions should be asked such as:

- What is the potential for growth in the organization?
- How are the demographics of the constituents changing?
- Is the organization prepared to meet the needs of the community?
- Is our facility adequate to handle growing needs?
- If not, what must be done to improve facilities?

Many organizations will plan a daylong retreat for board and staff members to discuss these issues as the culmination of the planning process. The retreat should be facilitated by an independent party who will lead them through this process.

Once the organization reaches consensus that a campaign is in order, a steering committee is then appointed to begin the next step. Members of this steering committee for a campaign to build a building might include the following individuals:

- Board members.
- Staff members.
- Major donors.
- Individuals with experience in construction.
- Individuals with experience in fundraising.
- Individuals with financial experience.

The Planning Study

The planning study is an important step in the campaign process. This study is sometimes called a feasibility study. This term has more recently been used less often because its goals are more than the feasibility of the campaign. It should be a planning tool for the organization. Most organizations need to conduct such a study before launching the campaign. The study provides the organization with the means to assess both its internal readiness to do a campaign and the community's willingness to support it. A study generally takes about three to four months to complete, so be sure to allow sufficient time when planning a campaign. The study should be done by outside consultants for several reasons, among them:

- An objective viewpoint will be needed to analyze the internal readiness of the organization.
- Interviewees will generally be reluctant to speak frankly to a representative of the organization about its leadership and its case.
- A professional experienced in conducting studies will need to analyze the data and provide objective recommendations.

Assessing Internal Readiness for a Campaign

A capital campaign will be challenging for an organization that does not have its internal house in order. An internal assessment should be conducted by an individual who can look carefully at the infrastructure of the organization in order to prepare for a capital campaign.

Infrastructure includes:

- Staffing of the organization.
- Office systems, including software.
- Gift acceptance policies and office procedures.
- The level of involvement and commitment of the board and volunteers.

Staffing for a campaign is critical. No matter what the size of the organization, consideration must be given to the amount of time the campaign will take from the existing staff's time. This is an especially sensitive area for organizations that do not have a formal development office. Often a campaign director will be hired or a staff person may be pulled from current duties to manage the campaign. A word of caution: Someone must dedicate sufficient time to campaign coordination. This is not a task that can be done by a staff member "when he has time."

One of the elements that will make campaign management, reporting, and stewardship flow more efficiently is a good software package. The organization will need to access past giving history of donors and be able to use this donor history, combined with additional research, to qualify prospective donors and assign them to an appropriate solicitor. Donor history is an invaluable resource in preparing for a capital campaign because in most cases the major gifts will be given by those who are already supporting the organization. Even if the organization is new to fundraising, there is probably some history of involvement with the organization that should be tracked. This software package will also be used to track all information about the campaign, including donors, prospects, volunteers, pledge amounts, and restricted gifts.

In addition to staffing and software, internal policies and procedures must be assessed. The organization should have gift acceptance policies, which will provide staff and volunteers with guidelines on what types of gifts will be accepted during the campaign, from whom gifts will be accepted, how these gifts will be recognized, and, in some cases, how they will be disposed of.

In today's world, transparency is critical, especially in light of the Internal Revenue Service's report forms, which nonprofits must file annually. There may be individuals or companies from whom the organization would not want to accept a gift. For example, some organizations have policies that prohibit them from taking gifts from an alcohol or tobacco company or from companies that are not considered socially responsible.

It is also important to have policies about accepting and handling gifts of real property or other non-cash gifts. Internal procedures should also be in place for the accepting, recording, and acknowledging pledges and gifts received. For instance, who opens mail, photocopies checks, makes the bank deposit, and signs the acknowledgment letters? These procedures should be in place for all fundraising but will be especially important in the capital campaign because this may be the first time the organization has accepted multi-year pledges in addition to one-time gifts.

Board Commitment

Board commitment is one of the key areas that must be addressed before moving forward with a campaign. Has the board reached consensus that this campaign is needed and agreed on a preliminary goal for the campaign? Does the board understand its role, which will include a financial commitment as well as work on the campaign?

If some board members are not willing to make a commitment, either financially or with their time, they should be interviewed individually to determine the cause of their reluctance. If the majority of the board is not "on board," it may not be the right time for a campaign. If one or two board members are not supportive, they might be persuaded by other board members. It is usually best if extremely negative board members give up their seats on the board and allow others who can be more supportive of the campaign to join.

Community Assessment

Once the organization has determined it is internally ready to run a capital campaign, the next step is doing an external assessment of whether the community is willing and able to support the project. The consultant will work with the organization to determine the key players who will be interviewed during the study.

Generally, anywhere from 35 to 50 individuals will be interviewed. Sometimes it will be necessary to meet with more individuals due to the size or scope of the campaign. Occasionally, a study will involve fewer interviews if there is a very small goal or the organization is certain that some donors will make large gifts. Interviewing the *right* individuals is more important than the number of interviews.

Some categories of individuals who should be interviewed include:

- Top donors to the organization.
- Potential major donors for the organization.
- Key board members.
- Key staff people.
- Community leaders.
- Key volunteers.
- Political leaders, especially if it is anticipated that government support of the project will be requested.

During the interviews, the consultant will be asking interviewees:

- Their opinion of the organization.
- Their assessment of the strength of the case.
- Their propensity to make a major gift.
- Their willingness to serve in a leadership role in the campaign.
- Suggestions for other donors.
- Suggestions for campaign volunteers.

The consultants will then prepare a report for the organization's leadership outlining the qualitative and quantitative responses to the questions asked. They will make recommendations for moving forward with a campaign or not, along with a proposed time schedule for the campaign. If the consultant recommends that the organization is not ready for a campaign, suggestions will be included on what the organization needs to do to better prepare itself for a campaign.

Developing the Case for Support

One of the first steps in the campaign is to develop a "case for support" for this campaign. This is the first essential ingredient in effectively communicating the organization's needs to its constituents. A preliminary case for support needs to be developed before the planning study begins.

Consultants will need written materials that outline the organization's programs and the needs that will be addressed in this campaign to share with the individuals being interviewed. The preliminary case statement will then be refined during the study before being translated into a final case statement. Some of the key ingredients that will be in the case for support include:

- Mission.
- Vision.
- History.
- Current programs and services.
- List of board and staff.
- Financial information.
- Need for future growth.
- Plan for addressing future needs.
- Opportunities for the donor to participate in the vision.

It is essential to have the final case statement completed before attempting to develop campaign brochures and other materials. All campaign materials must be based on the case statement in order to present a uniform message to all constituents. Even though the materials may be different in format, the message must be the same. Once the final case statement is completed, it is then time to think about what kind of campaign materials will be effective.

Typical campaign materials developed from the case statement include:

- Grant applications.
- Individual donor proposals.

- Solicitation letters.
- Brochures.
- Pledge cards.
- Letters of intent.
- Letterhead and envelopes.
- Response envelopes.
- Website or Web pages.
- Press releases.
- Campaign newsletters.
- Speeches.
- Fact sheets.
- Question-and-answer sheets.
- Volunteer training materials.
- Phone scripts.
- Named gift opportunities forms.

Remember that different constituents will be attracted to different aspects of the campaign. Although the way the message is presented will vary according to donor needs and expectations, the message must be consistent in all campaign materials.

Structuring the Campaign

Once the planning study has been completed and the organization decides to proceed, the first step is to develop a campaign plan outlining the entire structure of the campaign. If the organization is working with a consultant, generally the consultant will draft the plan. If there is no consultant involved, the organization must allow sufficient time for staff members to develop the plan and must have confidence in staff members' ability to complete the task.

The campaign plan is the foundation for a successful campaign and will help the organization get off to a good start. The plan should include a brief overview of the process taken by the organization that led to the campaign. A key ingredient is the campaign organizational chart, showing all the various divisions and the number of volunteers that will be needed to participate in each division. Position descriptions for all volunteers should be included, along with a time line for each committee and an overall time schedule. The campaign budget is also part of the campaign plan. Additional volunteers should be recruited when the plan is completed. Once the volunteer cabinet is in place, they will review the plan and make suggestions for possible changes.

It will be critical to show volunteers a well-thought-out plan, and the time and monetary expectations that will be asked of volunteers. The principal group of volunteers that will be involved are members of the campaign cabinet, which includes chairs of all the various subcommittees that will be involved in the campaign.

Having the plan in place and assuring that it is followed will make any campaign flow more smoothly. The campaign plan is one of the essential building blocks of a successful campaign, as is the planning study. If an organization is on a tight budget, it may be wise for the organization to pay a consultant to develop the plan and then the organization can implement the plan on its own or with limited guidance from the consultant.

Campaign Volunteers

Once the campaign plan is in place, the organization can start recruiting additional volunteers to help implement the plan. Although the role of staff and board will be important during the campaign, the role of volunteers is critical to its success and should not be undervalued. All the information in Chapter 4 (Involving Volunteers) can be included in the capital campaign process.

A chairperson who is well known and respected in the community will be able to use his or her influence to recruit other community leaders. Often, hundreds of volunteers will be involved in a campaign. Although this sometimes sounds like a daunting task to staff and volunteer leadership, it can be accomplished easily if the organizational structure is in place from the beginning. Once all volunteers are recruited for each division, they will need to be trained in techniques of making the "ask." Even volunteers who have a great deal of campaign experience will need to attend strategy sessions and help develop the appropriate strategies to solicit prospects. Committees working on various divisions in most cases should be trained separately, because the approach to solicit a leadership donor will be very different from that of those in the small business division, for example.

The campaign cabinet needs to meet regularly. Whether it meets monthly, bi-monthly, or quarterly depends on the size and scope of the campaign. Subcommittees should meet individually between meetings of the campaign cabinet. It is very important to have regularly scheduled meetings in order for subcommittees to report on progress and discuss developments within the organization, the project, and the campaign. These meetings also serve to help motivate volunteers.

Identifying and Cultivating Donors

One mistake many organizations make is that they think they must find a whole new group of donors for their capital campaign because they do not want to ask their loyal donors to help again. However, a principle of fundraising is that the most likely donors to the capital campaign will be those who are already supporting the organization.

Some organizations think they can raise all the money they need for their capital project through grants. Grants may play an important part in the campaign process, but it is important to remember that more than 80 percent of all contributions to charitable organizations comes from individuals.

The first place to start is with the "family" of the organization: board, staff, and others close to the organization. It is crucial to have 100-percent board commitment before asking others to support the project. A staff appeal should also be held early in the campaign in order to show the public that the family of the organization has given its full support to the campaign.

If the organization has an annual giving history, the place to start is its donor records. Even those organizations that think they do not have alumni or a built-in constituent base will probably have a pool of prospects that are close to the organization. Many organizations have "alumni"—individuals who have received services or have given service to the organization. Those who have given blood, adopted animals, or used a library card are likely donors when the organization launches a capital campaign.

Volunteers are another good source of campaign donations. Many organizations hesitate to ask their volunteers for money, knowing that they are giving of their time. However, remember that an individual's time is often as precious as his or her money. If people are giving of their time, they are likely to support the organization financially as well. Companies from which the organization buys goods and services are another likely pool of prospective donors.

Making the "Ask"

The majority of gifts in a capital campaign will come through personal one-on-one solicitations. Asking for donations to a capital campaign follows the same principles and procedures as asking for major gifts in person, by phone, or through the mail. In most cases it is simply a matter of a bigger gift throughout a longer period of time. Following the guidelines in Chapter 8, Chapter 9, and Chapter 10 will guide the organization through this process.

Campaign Events

Although a capital campaign should not depend on special events to raise the needed money for the project, events are an important step in the campaign process. Volunteers and donors need to be cultivated, inspired, and recognized. Some typical events that will take place in the campaign are:

- Cultivation breakfasts, luncheons, dinners, and cocktail parties.
- A kickoff event.
- A groundbreaking event.
- A dedication and open house.

Cultivation will often be one on one and will be handled through the solicitation subcommittees. However, often it makes sense to hold a series of cultivation events designed to bring in small groups of individuals, usually with a common interest, to provide information about the project. Some examples of cultivation events have already been outlined in other chapters of this book and can be used effectively during a capital campaign as well.

Generally, the key event in a campaign is the kickoff event, which is usually the campaign's major event. The primary focus of the kickoff event is to announce the campaign, but other key components of the event are to recognize donors who have already made a contribution and to inspire new donors to the campaign. Kickoff events can range from a formal black-tie dinner to a cocktail party or a series of luncheons in different regions if the organization is statewide or national in scope.

Regardless of the type and location, it is important to remember that the kickoff event should not be held until more than half of the goal has been raised. Announcing a campaign prematurely can be the kiss of death for the campaign. The costs of the kickoff event should be included in the campaign budget, as there is usually no charge for attending. The plan is to get as many key donors to attend the event as possible. Whatever type of event the organization chooses, it should always be upbeat and inspirational.

The groundbreaking is another event the organization can celebrate. For some organizations, ground is not broken until the campaign has been completed. In these cases, the groundbreaking and victory celebration can be one in the same. For other organizations, groundbreaking is started during the campaign, and then the dedication and open house become the victory celebration. The timing of the project and the events should be carefully coordinated in the overall campaign calendar. An event committee is responsible for coordinating all the campaign events.

Campaign Publicity

The public relations subcommittee of the campaign cabinet is responsible for all the various public relations for the campaign. These may include:

- Campaign theme and logo.
- Campaign printed materials including brochures, letterhead and envelopes, response envelopes, letters of intent, fact sheets, and question-and-answer sheets.
- Campaign CD, video, DVD, PowerPoint presentation.
- Press releases.
- Campaign Website, which may include a Webcam tracking construction progress.
- Press conferences.
- Campaign speeches.
- Promotional items.

The public relations subcommittee usually works with the campaign consultant and a graphic designer to create the theme and design a logo. The brochures and other campaign materials are developed based on the case for support and need to be completed early enough in the campaign so the various committees can use them in their work. As with campaign events, it is important not to release information about the campaign too early in the process. Often pre-campaign publicity is planned to focus on the organization's programs and services without mentioning the actual campaign. When the campaign is launched publicly, there will be sufficient public interest in the project to ensure a successful campaign.

Donor Recognition

Recognition is an important facet of the capital campaign. Recognition can come in many forms. Listing donors in the organization's newsletter and annual report, issuing a press release about a major gift, or donor walls, bricks, and plaques are all ways of providing donor recognition. Special recognition events at which donors are publicly recognized for their contributions can also be effective. Remember, however, that some donors wish to remain anonymous, and their anonymity must always be ensured. Providing a place on the pledge card or letter of intent for donors to print their name exactly the way they wish to be recognized and a box where they can check if they want to remain anonymous are simple ways of ensuring that donors are recognized according to their wishes.

Life After the Campaign

The campaign is over, and generally the first thing staff is ready to do is to kick back and relax after the final campaign celebration. A well-deserved vacation, or at least a few days off, is probably a good idea. However, before the glow of a successful campaign fades, the organization should think about how it can "capitalize" on its success to build a stronger development program and stronger organization for the future.

One of the major benefits of a successful campaign is that it leaves the organization much stronger than it was prior to the campaign. The reasons for this are several, and they include:

- The campaign starts with an internal assessment and recommendations to strengthen the infrastructure of the organization will result.

- The increased public relations efforts during a campaign will result in a heightened awareness of the organization in the community.

- The involvement of volunteers in the campaign will provide future volunteer fundraisers for the organization's ongoing development efforts.

- Staff will benefit from working with a consultant and will gain knowledge and experience that will be an asset to them and the organization.

Soon after the end of a campaign, a debriefing should be held with the board, staff, and campaign volunteers to discuss what went right, what went wrong, what should be done differently next time, and how to build on the campaign's success to enhance the organization's development program.

The database system developed for the campaign must be maintained on an ongoing basis. Pledge reminders need to be sent out to ensure a good collection rate. Donor pledges should be tracked, and, when the pledge is paid, it may be time to invite donors to increase their annual giving. This may even be done while pledges are being fulfilled. Some organizations fear asking donors for additional funds. However, once donors have supported a major project, their level of interest in the organization as well as their level of commitment generally increases dramatically. Donors are more likely to support the organization on an ongoing basis, so they should be included in annual fund appeals as soon as they become part of the database system.

Staying in touch with donors on a regular basis and keeping them updated on the progress of the campaign and the project are important. Inviting all donors to the dedication and open house when the new facility is completed are steps that sometimes get overlooked. But remember: The key to successful fundraising is relationships, relationships, relationships. In order to build these good relationships, the organization needs to maintain good donor communications.

Also, campaign volunteers will have developed more awareness and commitment to the organization. Keeping campaign volunteers involved in the organization's ongoing development efforts can be a real boost to fundraising. Volunteers can help in the annual fund, major gifts programs, and planned giving campaigns, especially those who have been involved in making personal solicitations. They will have the training to be effective fundraisers because of their involvement in the campaign. Some of these volunteers might also be invited to serve on the board or the fundraising committee.

The board's role in the campaign may have been the first exposure they have had to the importance of their own giving. This commitment should be built upon in future annual appeals by starting every year's fundraising program with an annual board appeal. Through their involvement in the campaign, board members will have more experience and knowledge about fundraising so they can now be invited to get more involved in the organization's ongoing development efforts.

Increased public awareness of the organization during the campaign can help it tremendously. Media contacts should continue to be cultivated for their ongoing support of the organization. Getting stories in the newspaper about the increased services the organization is able to provide due to the successful campaign will help in future fundraising efforts.

For some organizations, a capital campaign may be a once-in-a-lifetime occurrence. Others will be ready for another campaign within a few years after the current one ends. Regardless of the organization's situation, do not miss out on the opportunity to build a stronger organization after the campaign ends.

If the organization has completed a successful capital campaign, every other part of its fundraising efforts becomes much easier.

Chapter 17
Collaboration

Collaboration is a key word in funding circles, particularly among foundations and other funders who want to get the most bang for their buck. There are many ways in which nonprofits can collaborate with other nonprofits and with for-profit companies.

Collaboration in Proposal Writing

Whether submitting proposals to government agencies, foundations, businesses, or individuals, collaboration is one way to increase the chances of having the proposal funded. Funding sources and nonprofit agencies are acutely aware that the need for services greatly exceeds the funds available. With more than a million nonprofits vying for what many experts see as a shrinking funding pot, creative approaches are needed.

The first step is to think about groups with which the organization is working now or would like to work in the future. Meet with representatives of these groups to discuss how clients would be helped if several organizations worked together. If a decision is reached that collaboration on a proposal is in order, then a meeting should be held with all the groups that would work on the proposal.

When collaborating on proposal writing, agree on which agency will be the lead agency. The lead agency would write the proposal and apply for the grant funds. Discuss the specific roles each agency would play if the grant were awarded.

Establishing an Advisory Committee

One effective collaboration mechanism is the establishment of an advisory committee. For example, when submitting a proposal for a job training program, the composition of the advisory committee might include:

- Public high school administrator.
- Vocational school administrator.
- Private high school administrator.
- Representative of a large business.
- Representative of a small business.
- High school youth.
- High school teacher.
- High school counselor.
- Employee who is a recent graduate.

If submitting a proposal for a teen pregnancy prevention program, the advisory committee would be quite different and might include:

- Hospital administrator.
- High school teacher.
- Ob-Gyn specialist.

- Religious leader.
- Teen club representative.
- Teen who has been pregnant.
- Female teen who has not been pregnant.
- Male teen who has fathered a child.
- Male teen who has not fathered a child.

Contact several groups, have them agree to name a representative to the advisory committee, and ask them to write a letter of support that includes confirmation that their representative will serve on the advisory committee.

Write a section of the proposal stating that as soon as the grant is received the advisory committee will meet. The first task of the committee would be to review the grant terms and to advise the participating agencies on steps to take to make the program effective. The advisory committee would then meet periodically during the funding period.

Interagency Collaboration

One effective way of collaborating is for the numerous social agencies that are helping members of the same family to work together. The social service delivery system is often extremely disjointed. A single individual may receive services from several different agencies, such as a church, a mental health agency, a health clinic, and an AIDS organization. A family may be receiving services from a variety of agencies. For example, in one family the grandmother is receiving services from an Area Agency on Aging counselor, the mother attends a mental health clinic, the teen is meeting with his or her high school counselor, and the toddler is enrolled in Head Start.

Because of the realization that the system is inefficient, a powerful argument for obtaining funding is to present a proposal supported by an entire community. For example, assume the agency is submitting a proposal to help teenagers stay in school.

Think how the agency would increase its chances for obtaining funding if the proposal would describe specific roles for the following groups:

- Employers.
- Law-enforcement authorities.
- Religious leaders.
- School officials.
- Youth-serving organizations (for example, Boy Scouts).

When submitting funding proposals, it is important to describe these relationships in specific terms. How would each of these groups help the service recipients?

The funding source is more likely to fund a proposal if it is made aware of the other agencies assisting the same individual or the same family. Not only should the text of the application describe the interrelationships, but each agency should also submit a letter that outlines the cooperation in more detail and supports the funding application.

Another effective method of collaboration is for several agencies providing similar services to cooperate. If six Area Agencies on Aging serving a particular county would jointly apply for funds, the likelihood of funding would increase. If several small municipalities would join together to request a grant for the purchase of equipment that can be shared, funding chances would improve. One small municipality might have difficulty obtaining funds for a training center for its police, fire, and emergency personnel, but 10 municipalities applying together would significantly increase funding chances.

Public-Private Partnerships

One important buzzword in the lexicon of collaboration is the formation of *public-private partnerships*. In this model, the nonprofit organization would be the applicant agency for funds. However, a variety of services would be provided by several groups in both the public and private sectors.

For example, the agency might be seeking grants to provide a program for underprivileged children. Whereas obtaining enough funding from a single source might be difficult, a public-private partnership might include:

- A business providing computers.
- A church providing meeting space.
- A university providing interns.
- A government agency providing funds.
- A private foundation providing funds.
- A bank providing funds.
- A service group providing volunteers.
- A school providing educational services.
- A hospital providing health services.
- Individuals providing scholarship funding.
- A specialty business such as a printer providing in-kind services.
- Local governments offering meeting and parking space.
- Amusement parks providing complimentary tickets.

Again, be as specific as possible when outlining what each agency would provide. Include a letter from each agency in the application confirming its participation.

Collaboration to Reduce Costs

One other effective result of collaboration is reduced costs:

- **Joint purchasing:** Often, substantial savings can be realized by bulk purchasing.
- **Staff sharing:** It may be highly beneficial for three small agencies to share a skilled bookkeeper, for example.
- **Joint training:** Six agencies developing joint training programs will always be more cost-effective than each one developing individual programs.

- **Joint conferences:** Often, one agency cannot afford the fee of a well-known speaker. Several cooperating agencies can share this cost.

- **Space sharing:** Many communities have been successful in locating a number of nonprofits in the same building. They can share costs for items such as copiers and other equipment, and they may be able to save funds by sharing a receptionist, a bookkeeper, or a publicity specialist.

Fundraising Collaboration

Many agencies are having great success in collaborating to raise funds. Several small agencies that would have a difficult time sponsoring a major fundraising dinner will find it much easier when six agencies join together to sponsor it.

Agencies can join together to cosponsor a benefit performance, flea market, golf tournament, or other special events when individual sponsorship would be risky. Agencies can join together to ask for funds from businesses or individuals. One agency would serve as the lead agency and would receive all the funds. The fundraising request would include how the funds would be distributed to the other cooperating nonprofits.

Collaboration Rules

Though collaborations can be profitable, they also can be stressful. Some tips to follow are the following:

- Make certain that individuals from every agency participating in the collaboration sit down together before any decisions are made. If an organization has doubts about participating, it should not participate.

- Everything must be in writing and signed by all parties. The responsibilities of each party must be spelled out in writing.

- Budgets must be clear and agreed to in advance.
- Agreements on sharing income or expenses must be stated in writing and agreed to by all parties.
- Include in the final document a procedure for third-party arbitration if there is a major disagreement.

Collaboration with other agencies and with other groups in the community may initially be time-consuming, but it will make a significant contribution to fundraising efforts.

Conclusion
Putting It All Together

What can be learned from reading this book?

If the organization thought fundraising was going to be easy, it has now learned that it is never easy, but that using common sense and a few basic fundraising principles helps. Unfortunately, the authors still have not found a way to raise large sums of money for nonprofit agencies without a great deal of hard work. Sorry.

Work diligently to meet your goals and you will succeed in raising the funds needed for your organization.

In reading this book, the word that stands out more than any other word is *plan*. First, begin by planning far in advance, at least a year before the agency needs the funds. Strategic planning is critical. Having an agency development plan and an action plan for each staff member, board member, and volunteer involved in fundraising is essential.

Decide what services the agency would like to offer in the next year. One way to begin is to review the services being offered now. What specific results have been achieved? How have the users of the service (clients, patients, mental health consumers, museum visitors, concert attendees) benefited from the services? What additional services are being considered?

Get input in an organized way from:

- Board members.
- Users of the service.
- Potential service users.
- The staff.

Then carefully think through the options, keeping the following questions in mind:

- How much would each potential new service cost?
- Could the agency obtain the qualified staff to provide additional services?
- Could it find the volunteers needed to provide the additional services?
- What are the different options for locating the funds needed to provide the additional services?

When developing a plan that incorporates the answers to these questions, have the board review, confirm, and approve these goals, because they will be helping to raise the money to fund these programs.

Perhaps the organization might develop several fundraising goals, such as:

- "To continue services at the existing level, we need to raise $_____."
- "To help meet the need for additional services to assist existing clients, we need to raise $_____."
- "To assist all individuals in the community who need our services, we must raise $_____."

The formation of a fundraising committee is critical. This committee will play a major role in creating and implementing the development plan. This committee will explore the fundraising options outlined in this book, including special events, asking for funds from individuals, businesses, and organizations, and submitting grant proposals.

One factor in deciding which strategies to pursue is an estimate of the hours of volunteer time that can be counted on to assist with the fundraising efforts. Another is the amount of staff time the agency can devote to fundraising efforts. Staff time is limited because staff members need to provide services to clients, but remember: "No money, no mission." Review the role of the board in fundraising. Analyze the infrastructure that is in place and review the areas in which support systems need improvement.

One other theme that is stressed throughout this book is relationship-building or networking. The organization is going to be able to raise substantially more funds if the funders, including government agencies, businesses, organizations, foundations, and individuals, know about the organization and its programs before they are asked for financial support.

Indeed, throughout this book we have stressed a three-step process. First, think through who the potential donors are. Identify the individuals, foundations, businesses, and government agencies that will be asked for funds. Second, plan carefully how to get them to learn about the program. Then, and only then, ask them for money.

Another key point to remember is that it takes money to make money! This is an old adage, but it is very true. The organization will need to make an investment in fundraising.

Here are some items that need to be budgeted:

- **Software:** A donor software package will be needed to manage donor records. This is critical if the organization is serious about raising money. Identify the many software options that are available. Make sure that training and support are available for everyone adding data to the system.

Check with other agencies that have used the same software to learn about their experiences. Include the staff members who will be using the software in the decision-making process.

- **Website:** A top-notch Website is essential. Though an offer from a well-meaning volunteer to develop the Website might sound tempting, the organization needs to invest in a professionally designed Website. It is essential that the Website be kept current.

- **Staffing:** As the program grows, the organization may find that it needs to hire at least a part-time development officer. Salary ranges will vary but a full-time experienced development officer will probably run in the same area, as any of your other top management staff members.

- **Consultants:** A consultant may be needed to lead training sessions and to help to implement special projects such as a direct mail, telephone, or capital campaign. In some cases, a consultant is a good choice because there are no payroll expenses to consider.

Each of the areas of fundraising, such as direct mail, telephone fundraising, and planned giving, will have its own budget. Events, in particular, may require significant investments up front.

The Event Budget

Once a decision is made on the event to be held, a budget should be developed for both income and expenses. Be certain that members of the event committee, board, and staff as well as the volunteers are all aware of the budget. It is important to understand the difference between gross and net revenues. Many individuals look at the money taken in at the event and forget to deduct the costs of running it.

Direct mail and telephone fundraising using professionals, as mentioned previously, may be quite expensive. Other fundraising areas such as major gifts, planned giving, and volunteer phonathons typically have limited expenses except for staff time and materials to be used in soliciting donors. Capital campaigns, because they usually involve hiring a consultant, may seem to be more expensive to run, although compared to the size of the goal are often less costly than other types of fundraising that yield smaller amounts of money.

Capital Campaign Budget

There are two budget areas that must be considered when embarking on a capital campaign: the project budget and the campaign budget.

If the project involves construction, the architect or construction manager will generally help develop the budget for the building project itself.

If the organization is raising funds to build a building, campaign expenses and the building project expenses are recorded seperately. Campaign expenses are usually paid out of funds raised for the campaign. These expenses are dependent on many factors, such as the fundraising goals, the duration of the campaign, the geographic scope of the campaign, the time required from a consultant, and the existing fundraising structure in place within the organization.

These campaign costs include:

- Campaign personnel.
- Consultants.
- Marketing expenses.
- Donor recognition items and events.
- Campaign events.
- Support systems (software, telephone, fax, Internet, postage and office supplies).
- Travel expenses.

The campaign budget should be developed during the campaign planning phase and monitored on a monthly basis.

In Summary

All of this planning and thinking takes time. That is why the organization must start the process far in advance of when the funds are needed and the process never ends. Like the painting of the bridge, "forever fundraising" is a continuous process.

The good news is that it actually gets easier:

- Many givers continue to give in succeeding years because they support the mission of the organization.

- Volunteers give more time and recruit their friends to volunteer because they are excited about the program and feel valued and appreciated.

- Volunteers usually become financial supporters once they become committed to the organization's mission.

- Businesses think of additional ways to help once they have been involved in the planning process.

- Government agencies and foundations often fund the program continuously once they see its effectiveness in solving community problems.

In case anyone missed the message: **Planning is critical! Networking is essential! Diversification of funding is necessary!**

Focus on the mission. Do not get caught in "mission drift." Never give up! Remember the key words in fundraising are *planning* and *relationships.*

Thank you for continuing to serve your community.

Appendix A
Questions and Answers

The more workshops we lead, the more questions we get. Here are some of the most commonly asked questions about fundraising, and our answers.

Q: When should our organization hire a fundraising consultant? What process should we use if we decide to hire a consultant?

If the organization has the expertise and time to raise the required funds, there may not be a need for a consultant. If the nonprofit requires ongoing assistance with its fundraising activities, it should consider hiring a staff member with fundraising expertise. However, if the organization decides that it needs specialized expertise (for example, planned giving, board development, or grant writing), then hiring a consultant should be considered. Often, if the need is immediate—the organization needs to raise $2 million to build a building—retaining a consultant is the way to go.

The first step is to realistically outline the expertise and availability of staff members, board members, and other volunteers. Decide what specific service the consultant should provide. The general rule is that if your staff can provide these services, do not ask the consultant to provide them.

The first place to look for a consultant is with other organizations that have used consultants. Contact your colleagues to get recommendations both in your community and in other locations. If they have used a consultant, ask what were the positive and negative results of dealing with this consultant. Other places to find reputable consultants include local associations of nonprofits, the Association of Fundraising Professionals, or Internet searches. Once you develop a list of three or four firms you think will meet your needs, ask each prospective consultant for a written proposal. Request contact information for at least three clients for whom the consultant has worked. Ask for a fee schedule. Reputable consultants will either charge by the hour or by a set fee for a specific task. Do not deal with consultants who charge a percentage of the funds raised. Many states require that consultants be registered in order to provide fundraising services, so be sure to check with your state regulatory authorities and ask the consultant if his or her company is registered to provide services in your state.

Interview the prospective consultants in person. Include the executive director and the chair of the fundraising committee or board chair in the interview as well as anyone else who will be dealing with the consultant on a regular basis. Make certain to interview the individual who will be assigned to the project if you award the contract to the firm.

Make certain the contract includes the consultant's specific duties, terms of payment, and expectations the consultant has of the organization. A provision that the agency can cancel the contract at any time should also be included. Some states require approval of contracts and may include other requirements. For example, many states prohibit fundraising counsel from handling money for your organization.

Q: What if my board is just not interested in fundraising?

This is a common problem, so do not feel you are unique. Begin with one board member who "gets it," perhaps the board chair or a board member who is a philanthropist. Together with that individual, begin by analyzing why the board has this attitude. This individual should then lead a discussion about fundraising with the board at the next board meeting.

Some board members refuse to ask others for money. The discussion leader should explain that there are numerous ways of participating other than selling tickets or asking for donations. Board members should be given a list of the many ways they can help.

Let board members know when they join the board what is expected of them. This would include giving a contribution to the agency and attending special events. Give board members as much notice as you can of special events so they can put the dates on their calendars.

Explain to board members that, because they believe in the mission of the agency, their participation in fundraising is essential to meeting the needs of the individuals the agency is serving. Every agency must engage in "forever fundraising" to meet the needs of the community.

If particular board members do not meet their fundraising duties, the board chair should speak to them privately. If their nonparticipation continues, do not nominate them for another term at the end of the current one.

Q: I get very nervous when I go to someone's house or office to ask him or her for funds. What can I do to prepare?

It is normal to be apprehensive the first time you are doing anything. Make certain to participate in a training program so that you can get hints from more experienced fundraisers.

Learn about the agency so you can answer questions. What specific services can be offered if the agency's fundraising goals are met?

Learn as much as you can about the potential donors you are visiting. What have been their contacts with the agency? Have they supported the agency in the past, and, if so, at what level? Do they have any special interests or hobbies? Have they made gifts to other agencies in the community? Where did they attend school?

Engage in role-playing before the visit so that you will feel more comfortable. Role-play one scenario in which the prospect is positive and pledges a large amount. Then role-play in that the prospect is not cooperative and does not make a pledge.

Set up the appointment when you can meet with all the decision-makers in the home. When you enter the home, look around. Make a note of family pictures, hobbies, and special books or artwork. Begin by giving a brief overview of what specific services the agency can provide. Then ask the prospective donor a question about his or her connection with the agency or its mission.

As an alternative, ask the individuals to discuss their families, current events, or the artwork or book you have noticed. Learn to keep quiet! Let them talk! At the appropriate time, thank them for their support of the community and ask if they would make a generous pledge to your agency. Suggest an amount that is the largest amount you think they might contribute. Once they make a pledge, have them sign a pledge card and thank them.

Be aware that, the larger the gift, the more time my be required to make the decision. Often you will have to return to the home before a large pledge is made.

You will find that once you have made the first visit, it will get easier and easier. If you are really apprehensive the first time, ask a more experienced fundraiser to accompany you.

Q: We have had numerous volunteers who did not meet their responsibilities. What can we do to increase the number of responsible volunteers?

Lots of things. First, select volunteers carefully. Give as much thought to "hiring" volunteers as you do to hiring paid staff. Interview each potential volunteer. Give each a job description outlining their duties. If they do not seem as though they will make excellent volunteers, do not give them an opportunity to volunteer.

Make sure all volunteers participate in a two-part training program. The first part would include general information about the agency. The second would outline specific duties and how they should be performed.

Make it clear to volunteers that they have full freedom to volunteer for tasks they would like to undertake. If they are not comfortable in a fundraising position, maybe there are other opportunities within your organization for them to volunteer.

Special opportunities should be taken to thank volunteers for their services. Some should be personal. For example, volunteers should be thanked in person and in writing for their help. The agency should hold formal volunteer appreciation events from time to time as well.

Q: How do I word our fundraising appeal to increase the funds we receive?

Begin by discussing the programs your agency operates. List the specific programs the community is likely to support financially. Generally, it is easy to raise funds for programs that help children. It is easy to raise funds for victims of natural disasters. On the other hand, it is difficult to raise funds for individuals that donors may not think are worthy of support. Raising money for programs that help prisoners, for example, may be more of a challenge. Regardless of the cause, telling a personal story is always more persuasive than citing statistics.

In your fundraising materials, describe one or two programs that funders are likely to support. Give an example of a past success story. Perhaps an individual who was cured of a disease with the help of the agency can tell his or her story.

Be specific as to what the agency can accomplish if the fundraising goals are met. Word your appeal from the perspective of the donor. For example, state that "Your gift can help train 50 unemployed individuals to apply for available jobs in the community."

Make sure the fundraising letter or brochure is worded in understandable language and is free of agency jargon. Use pictures. If financial information is included, use simple pie charts rather than complex financial information.

Read it carefully. If you received such an appeal, would you write a check?

Q: We have not been successful in getting grants. What can we do to increase our chances?

Write one large grant outlining all the funds your agency needs. Then research all the different possible sources for these funds.

Diversification and *relationships* are the key words. Consider submitting applications to government agencies, foundations, businesses, and individuals. Apply to several sources for the funds you need. Before applying, research the interests of each funder to see if they match your programs.

Try to meet face to face with representatives of as many funding sources as you can. Larger foundations often have program officers who will meet with you. If the foundation is a family foundation, meeting with individual trustees is important if you want to get funded. For proposals to a corporate foundation, try to meet first with a representative of that business. Ask to meet with a staff person at every government agency to which you are thinking of applying. Ask the individual with whom you are meeting specific questions to help you submit a "winning" application for funding. Make sure to follow the instructions of the funding source.

Finally, read all grant applications carefully and also have them read by someone who is not familiar with your agency. It is the grant application interesting and convincing? Would you fund it?

Q: I've heard that a capital campaign takes years to complete. What if we do not have a lot of time?

Typically, a planning study will take three to four months to complete. This may seem like a long time, but the information obtained in the study is critical for most organizations.

Once the study is completed, the campaign itself typically runs from one to three years, depending on the amount of the goal, the size and geographic area of the organization's constituency, and the internal readiness of the organization to run a campaign. For some organizations, such as a religious institution for which most of the funds will be raised from within its own membership, the time to run a campaign is usually considerably shorter, often as short as six months, as there is no need to identify and cultivate potential donors.

If your organization has a critical need for a new building, you may want to consider obtaining some short-term financing while you raise the money. You must be aware, however, that running a campaign for debt financing is the most challenging way to raise money. However, many organizations start their campaign and obtain some type of "bridge loan" while pledges are being paid, so there is no need to wait until the pledge period is complete before starting construction.

Plan ahead is the best advice we can give you. If your organization is even remotely considering future expansion within the next three years, now is the time to start your strategic planning and complete your planning study. You should start by talking with an architect and a fundraising consultant. They will help you develop a calendar and coordinate the process of building construction and raising the money on a side-by-side time line.

Q: I would like to learn more about fundraising. Where do I start?

Numerous publications expand on the topics covered in this book. A list of resources is included in Appendix B. Join a professional association such as the Association of Fundraising Professionals (AFP). One feature that is amazing about the nonprofit community is their willingness to share with fellow professionals. The education, networking, and resources available at these meetings, workshops, and conferences are extensive. Of course, use the Internet. It contains a wealth of knowledge on this topic.

Find a mentor. An individual who has been in this field for a number of years can be an invaluable asset for the novice fundraiser. Some AFP chapters have formal mentoring programs as well.

Appendix B
Books You Might Find Helpful

Strategic Planning for Nonprofit Organizations
Michael Allison and Jude Kaye

Financial & Strategic Management for Nonprofit Organizations
Herrington Bryce

Donor-Centered Fundraising
Penelope Burk

Fundraising Basics: A Complete Guide
Barbara Ciconte and Jeanne Jacobs

Nonprofit Management Handbook
Edited by Tracey Daniel Connors

Conducting a Successful Capital Campaign
Kent Dove

Beyond Fundraising
Kay Sprinkle Grace

The Nonprofit Handbook
Gary Grobman

The Nonprofit Internet Handbook
Gary Grobman and Gary Grant

Fundraising
Jim Greenfield

The Law of Fundraising
Bruce Hopkins

Starting and Managing a Nonprofit
Bruce Hopkins

Governing Boards
Cyril O. Houle

Giving USA
Institute for Giving

Give to Live
Doug Lawson

The Development Plan
Linda Lysakowski

Recruiting and Training Fundraising Volunteers
Linda Lysakowski

Pinpointing Affluence
Judith Nichols

The Fundraising Feasibility Study: It's Not About the Money
Edited by Martin Novom

Board Room Verities
Jerold Panas

Born to Raise
Jerold Panas

Mega Gifts
Jerold Panas

Achieving Excellence in Fundraising
Henry Rosso

How to Manage an Effective Nonprofit Organization
Michael Sand

Developing Your Case for Support
Timothy Seiler

Careers in Fundraising
Lilya Wagner

Fundraising as a Profession
Lilya Wagner

Fundraising on the Internet
Mal Warwick, Ted Hart, and Nick Allen

Appendix C
Glossary

Here are a few terms you may hear in the field of fundraising. Adapted from the Association of Fundraising Professionals (AFP) Dictionary of Fundraising Terms.

Acquisition mailing: a mailing to prospects for acquiring new members or donors.

Address correction requested: a service provided for a fee by the United States Postal Service. A printed statement on a carrier envelope alerts post offices to provide correct address information to the organization listed as the return address.

Advanced Certified Fund Raising Executive (ACFRE): a credential earned by an individual who meets specific requirements, including previous certification (see **Certified Fund Raising Executive**). This credentialing process was developed and is administered by the Association of Fundraising Professionals.

Advisory board: a group of influential and knowledgeable individuals that offers counsel and prestige to the organization or cause with which it is associated but that usually does not have any fiscal or policy authority.

Annual giving: a fundraising program that generates gift support on a yearly basis.

Annual report: a yearly report of the financial and program status of an organization or institution.

Anonymous gift: a gift not publicly attributed to the donor.

Appeal letter: a letter requesting a donation to a fundraising campaign.

Articles of incorporation: a document that, when filed with and approved by an appropriate state agency, establishes the legal status of a corporation.

Association of Fundraising Professionals (AFP): a professional society (headquartered in Arlington, Virginia) that fosters the development and growth of fundraising professionals, works to advance philanthropy and volunteerism, and promotes high ethical standards in the fundraising profession. (Formerly the National Society of Fundraising Executives.)

Board profile: an analysis, study, review, and overview of the individual members of a governing board or an advisory board, including their skills, experience, and professional and social connections.

Board rotation: a term-of-office schedule that provides for a periodic succession.

BRE: business-reply envelope.

Bricks-and-mortar campaign: a capital campaign to meet the financial needs for constructing a physical plant, including facilities and furnishings.

Bulk-rate mail: second-, third-, or fourth-class mail that qualifies for special postage rates that are lower than first-class rates. This mail is presorted by an organization or a service before going to the post office.

Campaign cabinet: a group, including chairperson and other members of the group, that determines campaign policy and monitors campaign progress.

Capital campaign: an intensive fundraising effort to meet a specific financial goal within a specified period of time for one or more major projects that are out of the ordinary, such as the construction of a facility, the purchase of equipment, or the acquisition of endowment funds.

Carrier envelope: an envelope containing an appeal letter and other material that is attached to a direct-mail package.

Case: the reasons why an organization both needs and merits philanthropic support, usually outlining the organization's programs, current needs, and plans.

Case statement: a presentation that sets forth a case.

Cause-related marketing: marketing in which a for-profit organization, by using the name of a nonprofit organization, promotes its product and in return provides financial support to the organization according to a predetermined formula based on sales and purchases.

Certified Fund Raising Executive (CFRE): a designation, conferred by Certified Fund Raising Executive International, that is awarded to a professional fundraiser who has met specified standards of service, experience, and knowledge.

Certified public accountant (CPA): an accountant who has fulfilled the legal requirements for a state certificate to maintain and audit accounts and to prepare reports in tax and finance.

Charitable deduction: the portion of a gift to a qualified charity that is deductible from an individual's or a corporation's federal income tax, an individual's gift tax, or an individual's estate tax.

Charitable foundation: a corporation or trust set up and operated exclusively for charitable purposes. It may be established for the support of a particular charity, or it may make grants to multiple charities.

Chief development officer (CDO): the highest-ranking development staff member responsible for a development program.

Chief executive officer (CEO): the highest-ranking executive responsible for organizational operations.

Chief financial officer (CFO): a senior staff member responsible for the financial management of an organization, including budget control, cash-flow management, financial forecasting, and related functions.

Community foundation: a nonprofit organization that receives, manages, and distributes funds, including any income from endowed funds, for charitable purposes, typically in a specific geographic area.

Corporate foundation: a private foundation that is funded by a profit-making corporation and has as its primary purpose the distribution of grants according to established guidelines.

Corporate sponsorship: financial support of a project by a corporation in exchange for public recognition and other benefits.

Cultivation event: a special event (such as a dinner or similar event) to enhance interest in and enthusiasm for the work of an organization.

Database: indexed information held in computer storage from which a computer user can summon selected material. In a database, data are organized so that various programs can access and update information.

Deferred gift: a gift (such as a bequest, life insurance policy, charitable remainder trust, gift annuity, or pooled-income fund) that is committed to a charitable organization but is not available for use until some future time, usually the death of the donor.

Development: the total process by which an organization increases public understanding of its mission and acquires financial support for its programs.

Development audit: an objective evaluation, sometimes conducted by a professional fundraising consultant, of an organization's internal development procedures and results.

Development committee: a group of volunteers responsible for providing leadership, supervision, and the overseeing of an organization's fundraising program.

Development office: the department or division of an organization responsible for all facets of its development program.

Development plan: a written summary of development goals and objectives and the strategies by which an organization will achieve them within a given period of time.

Direct mail: mass mail sent by a nonprofit organization directly to prospects.

Director of development (DOD): an individual who manages the development programs of an organization.

Donor Bill of Rights: the statement of rights provided to a donor.

Electronic funds transfer (EFT): a process or act by which an individual may authorize automatic and periodic deductions from his or her bank account to be credited to another account, as to a nonprofit organization.

Endowment: a permanently restricted net asset, the principal of which is protected and the income from which may be spent and is controlled by either the donor's restrictions or the organization's governing board.

Executive director: an individual who manages or directs an organization's affairs.

Fact sheet: a brief statement of an organization's purposes, programs, services, needs, plans, and other pertinent information prepared in summary form for use by volunteers involved in a campaign.

Fair market value (FMV): for the purpose of establishing the value of non-cash gifts, the valuation of property based on what a willing buyer might pay to a willing seller for the property, or the value placed on a benefit or premium received as a result of a donation, ticket, or event.

Family foundation: a foundation funded entirely by one family.

Feasibility study: an objective survey, usually conducted by a fundraising consultant, of an organization's fundraising potential. The study assesses the strength of the organization's case and the availability of its leaders, workers, and prospective donors. The written report includes the study findings, conclusions, and recommendations.

Fiscal agent: a tax-exempt organization that manages funds or acts in a similar capacity for another tax-exempt organization.

Fiscal year: of an organization or government, the time between one yearly settlement of financial or taxing accounts and another.

501(c)(3): the section of the Internal Revenue Service code that exempts certain types of organizations (such as charitable, religious, scientific, literary, and educational) from federal taxation and permits these organizations to receive tax-deductible donations. For information about other 501(c) organizations, see the IRS Tax Code.

Foundation: an organization created from designated funds from which the income is distributed as grants to nonprofit organizations or, in some cases, to individuals.

Fundraiser: an individual, paid or volunteer, who plans, manages, or participates in raising assets and resources for an organization or cause.

Fundraising: the raising of assets and resources from various sources for the support of an organization or a specific project.

Gift-acceptance policy: the rules and regulations developed by an organization to determine which types of gifts should or should not be accepted.

Governance: a process by which decisions on policy, budget, and personnel are made by the board of an organization.

Grant: a financial donation given to support a person, organization, project, or program. Most grants are awarded to nonprofit organizations.

Grantee: a person or organization receiving a grant.

Honorary chair: a person of prominence or influence who agrees to lend his or her name to a campaign.

Independent sector: any nonprofit or tax-exempt organizations collectively that are specifically not associated with any government, government agency, or commercial enterprise.

Indicia: markings printed on bulk mail in place of stamps, metered postage, or other postmark.

L-A-I (Linkage, Ability, Interest): the three factors, when considered together, that are indicators of the likelihood of success when soliciting a major gift. Linkage is the association with an organization or constituency; ability is the capacity for giving; interest is the concern about the cause, need, or project.

Lapsed donor: a donor who has contributed at any time prior to the current year.

Leadership gift: a gift donated at the beginning of a campaign that is expected to set a standard for future giving.

Letter of intent: a declaration stating a person's intention to make a gift or bequest. In some states such a letter constitutes a legal obligation.

List broker: a commercial firm that buys, sells, and rents mailing lists.

List exchange: the exchange of constituent lists between two or more organizations, often on a name-for-name basis, that enables each organization to mail to the other's constituency.

Long-range plan: the goals and objectives of an organization that are based on a projection of existing conditions and trends and translated into budgets and work programs.

Mail house: a commercial business that addresses, inserts, sorts, bags, and delivers a mailing to a post office.

Mailing package: a package that usually contains an appeal letter, a brochure, and a response device.

Major gift: a significant donation to a nonprofit organization; the amount required to qualify as a major gift being determined by the organization.

Matching gift: a gift by a corporation matching a gift contributed by one or more of its employees, or a gift by a donor matching a gift contribution by a group of other individuals.

Memorial gift: a gift in commemoration of a deceased individual.

Mission statement: a statement about a societal need or value that an organization proposes to address.

990: an Internal Revenue Service financial information return submitted annually by most tax-exempt organizations and institutions except religious organizations.

990-PF: an Internal Revenue Service information return submitted annually by private foundations, reporting on their holdings, income, grants, and activities.

990-T: an Internal Revenue Service tax return submitted annually by nonprofit organizations to declare any unrelated business income.

Nonprofit postage rate: a special, reduced rate of postage accorded to a qualifying nonprofit organization.

Objective: a measurable step toward the achievement of a goal.

Operating foundation: a private foundation that, rather than making grants, conducts research, promotes social welfare, and engages in programs determined by its governing body or establishment charter.

Philanthropy: love of humankind, usually expressed by an effort to enhance the well-being of humanity through personal acts of practical kindness or by financial support of a cause or causes, such as a charity, mutual aid or assistance (service clubs, youth groups), quality of life (arts, education, environment), and religion.

Phonathon: a telephone campaign.

Planning study: a fundraising study that places emphasis upon the development of a plan to implement a campaign.

Pledge: a promise that is written, signed, and dated, to fulfill a commitment at some future time; specifically, a financial promise payable according to terms agreed to by the donor. Such pledges may be legally enforceable, subject to state law.

Pledge card: a printed form used by a donor as a response to an appeal.

Pledge payment: payment of all or a portion of a pledge.

Press release: an official statement (such as a story, item, or other announcement) issued to the media for publication.

Private foundation: as designated by federal law, a foundation whose support is from relatively few sources and typically from a single source (usually a person, family, or company) that makes grants to other nonprofit organizations rather than operating its own programs. Its annual revenues are usually derived from earnings on investment assets rather than from donations.

Private inurement: the receiving (by such as a board member, staff member, stockholder, or business owner) of financial benefit of the net profits from an endeavor. Nonprofit organizations cannot legally provide private inurement to any entity.

Pro bono: commonly used to designate work done without charge by a professional.

Proposal: a written request or application for a gift, grant, or service.

Prospect: any potential donor whose linkages, giving ability, and interests have been confirmed.

Prospect research: the continuing search for pertinent information on prospects and donors.

Prospect screening: a preliminary evaluation of broad categories of potential donors prior to rating.

Public-service announcement (PSA): an announcement promoting a nonprofit organization, program, or cause placed in print or broadcast without charge or fee.

Quasi endowment: an endowment from which the funds, both principal and interest, may be expended at the discretion of the governing board.

Request for proposal (RFP): an announcement issued by an organization seeking delivery of goods or services according to specifications.

Response device: a form or envelope used for conveying a reply to a mailed appeal.

Role-playing: in fundraising, the coaching of volunteers by having them perform the roles of solicitor and prospect in preparation for an actual solicitation.

SASE: a self-addressed, stamped envelope.

Site visit: a visit by a potential donor to inspect a project or review a program for which donations are being sought.

Special event: a function designed to attract and involve people in an organization or cause.

Stakeholder: a person (such as a volunteer, client, donor, or employee) who has a special interest in the activities and decisions of an organization.

Steering committee: a committee of top volunteer leaders who oversee and manage a campaign or other fundraising effort.

Stewardship: a process whereby an organization seeks to be worthy of continued philanthropic support, including the acknowledgment of gifts, donor recognition, the honoring of donor intent, prudent investment of gifts, and the effective and efficient use of funds to further the mission of the organization.

Strategic plan: decisions and actions that shape and guide an organization while emphasizing the future implications of present decisions. This plan usually employs the SWOT analysis.

Suspect: a possible source of support whose philanthropic interests appear to match those of a particular organization, but whose linkages, giving ability, and interests have not yet been confirmed.

SWOT analysis (strengths, weaknesses, opportunities, threats): an integral component of a planning process that examines an organization's internal strengths and weaknesses, and the external opportunities and threats that will impact its program in the market or markets in which it operates.

Technical-assistance grant: a grant providing an outside consulting service to an organization.

Telemarketing: the raising of funds or the marketing of goods or services by volunteers or paid solicitors, using the telephone.

Telethon: a television program in which entertainment features are integrated with a fundraising message that is broadcast over a television station. During the program, viewers are asked to call and make pledges.

UBIT: unrelated business income tax.

Unrestricted gift: a gift made without any condition or designation.

Vision statement: a statement about what an organization can and should become at some future time.

Appendix D
Typical Segment of a Development Plan

Goal	Objective	Strategy	Area of Responsibility	Budget	Time-line
I. Increase the board's involvement in fundraising	A. Establish a Development Committee	Appoint a Development Committee Chair from the board	Director of Development/ Board Chair	N/A	6/30/yy

Goal	Objective	Strategy	Area of Responsibility	Budget	Time-line
		Develop a position description for Development Committee	Director of Development/ Consultant/ Development Commitee Chair	$500 for consultant	7/31/yy
		Develop a list of 20 potential Development Committee members from the board and outside sources	Director of Development/ Consultant/ Board of Directors	$500 for consultant	8/31/yy
		Develop volunteer recruitment packet	Director of Development	$100 for folders and materials	8/31/yy
		Recruit at least 10 Development Committee members	Director of Development/ Board Members/ Development Committee Chair	N/A	10/31/yy
		Conduct orientation meeting for Development Committee	Director of Development/ Consultant/ Development Commitee Chair	$500 for consultant	10/31/yy

Index

About the Authors

Michael A. Sand, Esq., is the founder of SAND ASSOCIATES, a nationwide management consulting firm. The firm specializes in providing consulting and training to nonprofit organizations. In addition to fundraising, the firm provides services in areas including grant writing, strategic planning, board development, volunteer management, and supervision. Mike is the author of *How to Manage an Effective Nonprofit Organization* (Career Press, 2005).

Mike received his undergraduate and law degrees from the University of Pennsylvania and a master's degree in public administration from Penn State University. In 1966, he began his career as a grant writer for Philadelphia's anti-poverty program. He then served as assistant director of Montgomery County's anti-poverty program, deputy director of the Pennsylvania Bureau of Consumer Protection, and administrator of the Law Bureau of the Pennsylvania

Public Utility Commission. He was named the first executive director of the Community Action Association of Pennsylvania.

Since forming SAND ASSOCIATES in 1979, Mike has led sessions throughout the country on more than 20 topics in nonprofit management. He has conducted more than one thousand workshops at conferences and for individual agencies, and has taught courses and workshops at eight universities. He lives in Harrisburg, Pennsylvania.

Linda Lysakowski, ACFRE, is President/CEO of CAPITAL VENTURE, a full-service consulting firm with offices throughout the United States. Linda is one of fewer than one hundred professionals worldwide to hold the Advanced Certified Fundraising Executive designation. She has managed capital campaigns ranging from $250,000 to more than $30 million, helped more than 100 nonprofit organizations achieve their development goals, and has trained more than 12,000 professionals in all aspects of development.

Linda is a magna cum laude graduate of Alvernia University in Reading, Pennsylvania. She is a graduate of the Association of Fundraising Professionals (AFP) Faculty Training Academy. She has served on the board of the AFP Foundation for Philanthropy and numerous other nonprofit and membership organizations.

She is a frequent presenter at regional and international conferences and has received two AFP research grants. Wiley Press has published her books *Recruiting and Training Fundraising Volunteers* (2005) and *The Development Plan* (2007). Linda is a contributing author to *The Fundraising Feasibility Study: It's Not About the Money* (Wiley, 2007). She lives in Las Vegas, Nevada.

To Contact the Authors

Ask Mike and Linda to help your organization. Both of our firms are full service. We can assist not only with fundraising campaigns but also in areas such as strategic planning and board development. No matter where you are located, we can help your organization grow and improve.

Contact us if you need help with:

- Fundraising.
- Board development.
- Board training.
- Strategic planning.
- A capital campaign.
- A development audit.
- A planning study.

- Development plans.
- Grant proposals.
- Grant management.

Visit our Websites to learn more about the ways we are helping hundreds of nonprofit organizations throughout the country overcome their challenges.

We look forward to working with you as part of our life goal of improving nonprofit agencies. Send us an e-mail or call us to tell us how we can help you.

Michael A. Sand, Esq.	Linda Lysakowski, ACFRE
MSand9999@aol.com	Linda@cvfundraising.com
(717) 238–5558	(866) 539–9990
www.sandassociates.com	*www.cvfundraising.com*